2003 SUPPLEMENT

CASES AND MATERIALS

FEDERAL INCOME TAXATION

FOURTH EDITION

by

PAUL R. MCDANIEL
Professor of Law
Boston College Law School

MARTIN J. MCMAHON, JR.
Clarence J. TeSelle Professor of Law
University of Florida

DANIEL L. SIMMONS
Professor of Law
University of California at Davis

FOUNDATION PRESS
NEW YORK, NEW YORK
2003

THOMSON
WEST

395 Hudson Street
New York, NY 10014
Phone Toll Free 1–877–888–1330
Fax (212) 367–6799
fdpress.com

Printed in the United States of America

ISBN 1–58778–620–6

PREFACE

The purpose of this 2003 Supplement to Federal Income Taxation, Cases and Materials, 4th Ed. is to provide users of the text with materials reflecting developments in federal income taxation since December 31, 1997 (the date as of which the materials in the text are current). This supplement is current as of April 30, 2003 and includes all significant Treasury Regulations, judicial cases, and Internal Revenue Service rulings promulgated after December 31, 1997 and before May 1, 2003, as well as all significant federal tax legislation enacted after December 31, 1997 and before June 1, 2003.

PAUL R. MCDANIEL
MARTIN J. MCMAHON, JR.
DANIEL L. SIMMONS

June, 2003

*

TABLE OF CONTENTS

*

TABLE OF INTERNAL REVENUE CODE SECTIONS

UNITED STATES

UNITED STATES CODE ANNOTATED

26 U.S.C.A.—Internal Revenue Code

UNITED STATES CODE ANNOTATED

26 U.S.C.A.—Internal Revenue Code

UNITED STATES CODE ANNOTATED

26 U.S.C.A.—Internal Revenue Code

UNITED STATES CODE ANNOTATED

26 U.S.C.A.—Internal Revenue Code

UNITED STATES CODE ANNOTATED

26 U.S.C.A.—Internal Revenue Code

UNITED STATES CODE ANNOTATED

26 U.S.C.A.—Internal Revenue Code

TABLE OF TREASURY REGULATIONS

TEMPORARY TREASURY REGULATIONS

PROPOSED TREASURY REGULATIONS

TREASURY REGULATIONS

*

TABLE OF CASES AND RULINGS

Principal cases are in bold type. Non-principal cases are in roman type. References are to Pages.

2003 SUPPLEMENT

CASES AND MATERIALS

FEDERAL INCOME TAXATION

*

PART I

INTRODUCTION TO FEDERAL INCOME TAXATION

CHAPTER 1

INTRODUCTION TO FEDERAL INCOME TAXATION

SECTION 1. AN HISTORICAL OVERVIEW

Page 13:

After the third full paragraph, insert:

K. 2001: THE NEW MILLENNIUM—REDUCING PROJECTED BUDGET SURPLUSES

In the last few years of the twentieth century, the federal government ran surpluses for the first time in more than thirty years. Projections by the Office of Management and Budget and the Congressional Budget Office estimated that over the first decade of the twenty-first century those surpluses could be substantial given certain optimistic assumptions regarding the continued growth of the economy. The year 2001 saw a Republican president and a Republican majority in both houses of Congress for the first time since the early 1950s. As result, in a highly partisan vote, Congress quickly enacted the Economic Growth and Tax Reconciliation Act of 2001, which in large part fulfilled the campaign promises of President George W. Bush. The changes in this Act were intended to reduce tax revenues by $1.35 trillion during the period from 2001 through 2010. The most significant provisions of the 2001 Act were a substantial reduction in income tax rates, and the complete repeal of the federal estate tax (but not the federal gift tax). Many of the amendments enacted in 2001 have delayed effective dates. To reduce the immediate budgetary impact of the drastic rate reductions, most of the income tax rate reductions are phased-in over five years and take full effect in 2006. Estate tax rates are scheduled to be reduced moderately, and the exemption will be increased significantly, between 2001 and 2009, with the estate tax to be completely repealed effective in 2010. For reasons having to do primarily with Congressional procedural rules, however, unlike most other modern amendments to the Internal Revenue Code, every amendment to the Code enacted in the Economic Growth and Tax Reconciliation Act of 2001 is scheduled to sunset on December 31, 2010. Thus, absent further Congressional action, on January 1, 2011, all of the changes implemented by the 2001 Act are automatically repealed and the Code reverts to its pre–2001 Act provisions. Some of the phase-in rules take so long that many provisions, such as the repeal of the estate tax, will be in full effect for only one year before they are scheduled to sunset. The political supporters of the 2001 Act are confident that future congresses will extend the amendments or make them permanent.

Later in 2001, following the terrorist attacks of September 11, 2001, Congress enacted the Terrorist Victims Relief Act of 2001, which provided targeted tax relief for victims of the terrorist attacks, and members of their families, and tax incentives for investments in the affected area of lower Manhattan or investments by businesses in that area. Most of the provisions were temporary; only a few permanent provisions affecting victims of future terrorist or military actions were enacted.

The year 2002 saw yet another tax act. The somewhat misleadingly named Job Creation and Worker Assistance Act of 2002 (not completely misnamed because it extended unemployment benefits) provided tax cuts for businesses through a series of new and extended accelerated depreciation deductions and credits for business expenses, as well as more tax benefits for businesses in New York City affected by the terrorist attacks.

In 2003 the Republican administration and Congress continued to fulfill their publicly stated intentions to enact a major tax reduction on an annual basis. The Jobs and Growth Tax Relief Reconciliation Act of 2003 accelerated the effective dates of a number of the income tax provisions enacted in the Economic Growth and Tax Reconciliation Act of 2001, most significantly, the reduction of the upper level income tax rates—particularly those that applied to the highest quintile of income earners. The 2003 Act also decreased corporate and other business taxes through preferential deductions (instead of expressly reducing corporate tax rates), and significantly reduced the tax rate on long-term capital gains—mostly stock market profits and profits from speculative investments in real estate. Finally, and most dramatically, the 2003 Act significantly reduced the tax rate on dividends received on corporate stock, taxing such dividends at the same preferential low rates that apply to long-term capital gains. Many of the changes in the 2003 Act are scheduled to sunset after three or four years, and those that are not scheduled for an earlier sunset, will sunset on December 31, 2010, like all of the changes in the 2001 Act. The sunset provisions of the 2003 Act exist for the same reasons as the sunset provisions in the 2001 Act. However, as with the 2001 Act, the political supporters of the 2003 Act are confident that future congresses will extend the amendments or make them permanent.

Independent analysis of the 2003 Act by the Institute on Taxation and Economic Policy (a non-profit, non-partisan research and education organization that studies government taxation and spending policy issues; http://www.ctj.org/itep/index.htm) found that over the next four years more than two-thirds of the tax reduction inures to the best-off 10 percent of all taxpayers, the top five percent will receive significantly more than one-half of the tax reduction, and the top one percent receives 39 percent of the tax reduction. Starting in 2006, after most changes other than the general rate reduction and the rate reduction for capital gains and dividends have sunset, the top one percent will receive 52 percent of the ongoing tax reduction. Over the next four years, the bottom 60 percent of taxpayers will receive only 8.6 percent of the tax reduction, averaging less than $100 a year, while the average tax reduction for the richest one percent will be $103,899. See http://www.ctj.org/pdf/sen0522.pdf.

L. WORLDWIDE PERSPECTIVE ON TAX BURDENS

The following table provides data by which the level of taxation in the United States, as a percentage of Gross Domestic Product, can be compared to the level of taxation in the other industrialized countries that are members of the Organization for Economic Cooperation and Development. This table, which reflects the most current comprehensive data available, reflects taxation by all levels of government, local as well as national, in the listed countries for selected years between 1975 and 2000.

TOTAL TAX REVENUE AS PERCENTAGE OF GDP

	1975	1985	1990	1995	1998	1999	2000 Provisional
Canada	33.1	33.6	36.6	36.6	38.3	38.2	37.5
Mexico		17.0	17.3	16.6	16.5	16.8	18.1
United States	26.9	26.1	26.7	27.6	28.8	28.9	n.a.
Australia	26.6	29.1	29.4	29.4	29.8	30.6	n.a.
Japan	20.9	27.5	30.7	27.9	26.8	26.2	27.1
Korea	15.2	16.9	19.1	20.5	22.9	23.6	26.4
New Zealand	31.1	33.6	38.0	38.0	35.5	35.6	36.2
Austria	37.7	41.9	40.4	41.6	44.2	43.9	43.3
Belgium	40.8	45.8	43.1	44.8	45.9	45.7	46.0

	1975	1985	1990	1995	1998	1999	2000 Provisional
Czech Republic				40.1	38.1	40.4	39.5
Denmark	41.4	47.4	47.1	49.4	49.5	50.4	48.4
Finland	37.7	40.0	44.7	44.9	45.9	46.2	46.5
France	36.9	43.8	43.0	44.0	45.1	45.8	45.5
Germany	36.0	32.9	32.6	38.2	37.0	37.7	37.8
Greece	21.0	28.6	29.3	31.7	35.7	37.1	38.0
Hungary				42.4	38.8	39.2	38.7
Iceland	29.6	28.1	31.0	31.2	34.1	36.3	37.3
Ireland	30.2	35.0	33.5	32.8	31.7	32.3	31.5
Italy	26.2	34.4	38.9	41.2	42.5	43.3	42.3
Luxembourg	39.0	44.4	40.5	41.7	41.1	41.8	42.0
Netherlands	43.0	42.4	42.8	41.9	40.9	42.1	41.8
Norway	39.9	43.3	41.8	41.5	43.4	41.6	40.2
Poland				39.6	37.6	35.2	n.a.
Portugal	21.2	26.9	29.4	32.5	33.5	34.3	34.7
Slovak Republic					37.1	35.3	35.8
Spain	19.5	27.6	33.0	32.8	34.1	35.1	35.3
Sweden	43.4	48.5	53.6	47.6	51.6	52.2	53.3
Switzerland	27.9	30.2	30.6	33.1	34.6	34.4	35.9
Turkey	16.0	15.4	20.0	22.6	28.4	31.3	32.8
United Kingdom	35.4	37.6	35.9	35.1	37.1	36.3	37.7
Unweighted average:							
OECD Total	31.1	33.8	35.0	36.1	36.9	37.3	
OECD America	30.0	25.5	26.9	26.9	27.9	28.0	
OECD Pacific	23.5	26.8	29.3	29.0	28.8	29.0	
OECD Europe	32.8	36.5	37.4	38.7	39.5	39.9	
EU 15	34.0	38.5	39.2	40.0	41.1	41.6	

Source: http://www.oecd.org/pdf/M00018000/M00018988.pdf

The data show that Mexico, Japan, and Korea are the only industrialized democracies with a lower tax burden than the United States. For many years Turkey had a lower tax burden than the United States, but in recent years that ranking has been reversed. For the most part, the higher tax burdens in other countries reflect a heavy reliance on consumption based taxes, such as a value added tax (VAT)—a tax roughly analogous in end result to a retail sales tax, although a VAT has a much more refined collection process—which relative to income taxes are borne more heavily by lower income individuals by than higher income individuals.

In considering this data it is important to keep in mind that the tax burden data of the OECD is based on the aggregate. The percentage of income paid as taxes by any individual (including taxes paid indirectly through corporate income taxes, employer wages taxes, etc.) varies widely within any country, although the preponderant determinant is the individual's income level (or in some cases the income level of the household of which the individual is a member). The following table, from Congressional

Budget Office, Effective Federal Tax Rates, 1979–1997 at 170, Table J–1 (Oct. 2001), shows the effective federal income tax rate for U.S. taxpayers in various income categories for the years 1995 through 1999.

EFFECTIVE FEDERAL INDIVIDUAL INCOME TAX RATE (PERCENT) BY ADJUSTED GROSS INCOME, 1995–1999

AGI Category	1995	1996	1997	1998	1999
$0 to $10,000	–5.8	–6.2	–6.1	–6.1	–5.9
$10,000 to $20,000	0.3	0.2	–0.2	–0.6	–0.5
$20,000 to $30,000	7.0	6.9	6.9	6.1	6.1
$30,000 to $50,000	9.9	10.0	10.0	9.3	9.3
$50,000 to $75,000	11.6	11.7	11.7	11.1	11.1
$75,000 to $100,000	14.0	14.2	14.1	13.6	13.7
$100,000 to $150,000	16.8	16.8	16.7	16.5	16.5
$150,000 to $200,000	19.6	19.7	19.5	19.2	19.3
$200,000 and Over	28.1	28.0	27.0	26.2	27.0
All Categories	13.5	14.0	14.2	14.0	14.6

These data reveal that taxpayers whose AGI is below $100,000 pay less than the aggregate average income tax rate, while taxpayers whose AGI is $100,000 or more pay more than the aggregate average income tax rate. In this regard it is important to understand that only 7.5 percent of tax returns reported AGI of $100,000 or more. Thus, 92.5 percent of all returns reflect an average income tax rate below the aggregate average income tax rate, while 7.5 percent of income tax returns reflect an average income rate above, the average income tax rate. It is also important to keep in mind that AGI is a figure that is far removed from many taxpayers' economic income. AGI is derived after excluding many items of income and deducting tax preferences for business investments. Thus, particularly in the upper income categories, the above data significantly overstate the effective rates for taxpayers in those categories.

SECTION 2. THE FEDERAL INCOME TAX SYSTEM

B. THE ADMINISTRATIVE PROCESS

(4) TAX COURT PROCEEDINGS

Pages 27 and 28:

Omit the sentence that begins on page 27 and ends on page 28, and after the carryover paragraph on page 28 insert:

Prior to 1998, the taxpayer bore the burden of proof in whatever forum tax liability was litigated. Under § 7491, enacted in 1998, however, the burden of proof is on the government in any *court proceeding* with respect to any factual issue with respect to which the taxpayer has introduced "credible evidence" if certain conditions set forth in § 7491(a)(2) have been satisfied. First, the taxpayer must have complied with any applicable substantiation or record keeping requirements imposed by the Code or Regulations. Second, the taxpayer must have cooperated with reasonable requests by the IRS for witnesses, information, documents, meetings, and interviews, and must have exhausted administrative remedies. This requirement will result in the burden of proof remaining on the taxpayer in cases involving nonfilers and other outright cheating cases, as well as in more routine cases in which the taxpayer simply fails to cooperate through dilatory and evasive tactics, of which there are large numbers of reported decisions. Furthermore, some taxpayers may conclude that the potential benefit of shifting the burden of proof is not worth the detriment of producing the required information before litigating the case. Finally, if the taxpayer is a corporation, partnership or trust, the taxpayer's net worth may not exceed $7,000,000. Once the basic qualifying conditions have been met, to shift the burden of proof to the government the taxpayer must introduce credible evidence relevant to establishing his tax liability. If the taxpayer fails to introduce any such evidence, the burden of proof remains on the taxpayer, and the taxpayer very likely will have failed to carry that burden of proof. In any event, § 7491 does not apply at all if any other Code provision specifies who bears the burden of proof.

Page 28:

In the second line of the third full paragraph, change "$10,000" to "$50,000."

(5) REFUND PROCEDURE

Page 29:

In the next to last line of the first full paragraph, replace "$1,000,000" with "$2,000,000".

(6) INTEREST, PENALTIES AND ATTORNEYS' FEES

Page 29:

Omit the second sentence of the final incomplete paragraph and insert:

Interest on refunds owed to individuals is likewise set at the short term federal rate plus three percent.

Page 32:

After the second full paragraph, insert:

The Commissioner always bears the burden of proof with respect to penalties and additions to tax. Section 7491(c), however, requires only that the Commissioner come forward with evidence that a particular penalty is appropriate. It does not require the Commissioner to prove that the taxpayer did not have "reasonable cause" or "substantial authority" for his position. The taxpayer must raise exculpatory circumstances that might negate application of penalty provisions. See H. Rep. No. 599, 105th Cong., 2d Sess. 58 (Conf. Rep. 1998).

Page 33:

In the eighth line of the first full paragraph, change "$110" to "$125."

SECTION 3. AN OVERVIEW OF POLICY ISSUES AND THE CURRENT INCOME TAX

C. THE STRUCTURE OF THE INCOME TAX AND SELECTED POLICY ISSUES

Page 59:

After the carryover paragraph, insert:

From 1993 through 2001, § 1 provided five marginal tax brackets: 15 percent, 28 percent, 31 percent, 36 percent, and 39.6 percent. The upper and lower parameters of each bracket were statutorily specified in terms of 1992 dollars, and were (and continue to be) adjusted for inflation. See I.R.C. § 1(f). The actual dollar denominated range of each bracket was (and continues to be) announced annually in a Revenue Procedure. The 2001 Act amended § 1 significantly. First, § 1(i) provides an initial 10 percent marginal rate bracket carved out of the broader 15 percent bracket specified in § 1(a)–(d). The upper limit of this new 10 percent bracket, however, is not adjusted for inflation for years before 2009. Second, the 2001 Act provided that beginning in 2001 (but effective only after June 30, 2001), the 28 percent, 31 percent, 36 percent, and 39.6 percent rates would be reduced according to the following schedule.

Taxable year	Rate to be substituted in § 1 for the 2000 rates:			
	28%	31%	36%	39.6%
2001	27.5%	30%	35%	39.1%
2002 & 2003	27%	30%	35%	38.6%
2004 & 2005	26%	29%	34%	37.6%
2006 and thereafter	25%	28%	33%	35%

In the 2003 Act, Congress accelerated the rate reduction by putting the 25 percent, 28 percent, 33 percent, and 35 percent brackets previously scheduled to take effect in 2006 into effect for all years after 2002.

The 15 percent bracket rate was not reduced, but the 2003 Act increased the size of the 15–percent regular income tax rate bracket for married taxpayers filing joint returns to twice the width of the 15–percent regular income tax rate bracket for single returns for taxable years beginning in 2003 and 2004. For taxable years beginning after 2004, the upper limit of the 15 percent rate bracket for married taxpayers filing joint returns reverts to the amount provided in § 1(a) and (f). The 2003 Act also temporarily accelerated an increase in the taxable income ceiling of the 10–percent rate bracket from $6,000 to $7,000, and for married taxpayers filing joint returns from $12,000 to $14,000 (indexed for inflation in 2004), previously scheduled to take effect in 2008, to be effective in 2003 and 2004. Starting in 2005, the taxable income ceiling for the 10–percent rate bracket reverts to the levels provided under the 2001 Act (which are not adjusted for inflation). See I.R.C. § 1(i).

As a result, starting in 2003 there are six rate brackets—10 percent, 15 percent, 25 percent, 28 percent, 33 percent, and 35 percent. The upper and lower limits of the brackets will change annually in patterns that are almost beyond description. This hodgepodge rate structure was adopted for budgetary and political reasons, and thus cannot be viewed as permanent. In fact, like all of the amendments to the Code in the 2001 Act, these changes sunset on December 31, 2010. Thus, absent further congressional action, in 2011 § 1 will revert to the five brackets in effect for 2000, with inflation adjustments in the dollar denominated bands. However, if the past is prologue, we can expect to see Congress enact changes to the rate structure, some temporary, others phased-in, on an almost annual basis for the foreseeable future. Whether any of the changes will be "permanent" is something no one can predict.

PART II

Gross Income

CHAPTER 2

General Principles of Gross Income

Section 2. Indirect Benefits

Page 68:

After the carryover paragraph, insert:

In civil tort litigation, damages awarded to a successful plaintiff typically are paid by the defendant to the plaintiff's attorney, who, in turn, remits the damage award or settlement minus the attorney's fees, which often are contingent fees, to the plaintiff. The payments on behalf of the plaintiff for attorney's fees may be viewed as third-party benefits includible in the successful plaintiff's gross income as a part of taxable damages under the principles of *Old Colony Trust*. There have been a number of cases in recent years addressing whether the portion of a taxable damage award retained by the taxpayer-plaintiff's attorney as a contingent fee is includible in the taxpayer's gross income under § 61, or whether the attorney's fees are excluded from the successful plaintiff's income and treated as income earned directly by the attorney. The issue is significant for affected taxpayers because, although the attorney's fees are deductible as a cost of earning a taxable damages award, the deductions are treated as miscellaneous itemized deductions that are limited to the amount in excess of two-percent of the taxpayer's adjusted gross income (discussed in the text at page 653). In addition, miscellaneous itemized deductions are not allowed as deductions in calculating the alternative minimum tax (Chapter 36). As a consequence, in some cases it is possible that the successful plaintiff's obligations for attorney's fees plus the tax incurred as a result of including the fees in the plaintiff's gross income may exceed the total amount of the judgment.

The Courts of Appeals have reached conflicting results on this question. In Kenseth v. Commissioner, 114 T.C. 399 (2000), which follows, the sharply divided Tax Court analyzed the split in the Circuit Courts and followed the majority view requiring inclusion of the entire amount of the damage award in the plaintiff-taxpayer's gross income.

Kenseth v. Commissioner*

United States Tax Court, 2000.
114 T.C. 399.

■ RUWE, JUDGE: Respondent determined a deficiency of $55,037 in petitioners' 1993 Federal income tax. The sole issue for decision is whether petitioners' gross income includes the portion of the settlement proceeds of a Federal age discrimination claim that was paid as the attorney's fees of Eldon R. Kenseth (petitioner) pursuant to a contingent fee agreement.

FINDINGS OF FACT

* * *

In a complaint filed with the Wisconsin Department of Industry, Labor, and Human Relations (DILHR) in October 1991, petitioner alleged that on March 27, 1991, APV Crepaco, Inc. (APV), terminated his employment. The complaint also alleged that, at the time of his discharge, petitioner was 45 years old, held the position of master scheduler, was earning $33,480 per year, and had been employed by APV for 21 years. It further alleged that, around the time of petitioner's discharge, APV did not terminate younger employees also acting as master schedulers but did terminate other employees over age 40.

Prior to filing the DILHR complaint, petitioner and 16 other former employees of APV (the class) retained the law firm of Fox & Fox, S.C. (Fox & Fox), to seek redress against APV. In July 1991, petitioner executed a contingent fee agreement with Fox & Fox that provided for legal representation in his case against APV. Each member of the class entered into an identical contingent fee agreement with Fox & Fox.

The contingent fee agreement was a form contract prepared and routinely used by Fox & Fox; the client's name was manually typed in, but the names of Fox & Fox and APV had already been included in preparing the form used for all the class members. Fox & Fox would have declined to

* The Tax Court's decision was affirmed, 259 F.3d 881 (7th Cir. 2001).

represent petitioner if he had not entered into the contingent fee agreement and agreed to the attorney's lien provided therein.

* * *

At the time of entering into the contingent fee agreement, petitioner had paid only the $500 "win or lose" retainer to Fox & Fox. This amount was to be credited against the contingent fee that would be payable if there should be a recovery on the claim; if there should be no recovery, this amount was nonrefundable. Under section II of the agreement, petitioner expressly agreed to reimburse Fox & Fox for out-of-pocket expenses * * *. In contrast, under section III of the agreement (which set forth the contingent fee agreement), petitioner did not expressly agree to pay anything. Instead, section III provided how the amount of the contingent fee was to be calculated if there should be a recovery. * * *

The contingent fee agreement required aggregation of the elements of any settlement offer divided between damages and attorney's fees and provided that any division of such an offer into damages and attorney's fees would be disregarded by Fox & Fox and petitioner. The contingent fee agreement provided that petitioner could not settle his case against APV without the consent of Fox & Fox. Under the contingent fee agreement, petitioner agreed that Fox & Fox "shall have a lien" for its fees and costs against any recovery in petitioner's action against APV. This lien by its terms was to be satisfied before or concurrently with the disbursement of the recovery. The contingent fee agreement further provided that, if petitioner should terminate his representation by Fox & Fox, the firm would have a lien for the fees set forth in section III of the agreement, and all costs and disbursements that had been expended by Fox & Fox would become due and payable by petitioner within 10 days of his termination of his representation by Fox & Fox.

* * *

On June 16, 1992, Fox & Fox filed a complaint on behalf of petitioner and the other class members against APV in the U.S. District Court for the Western District of Wisconsin. The complaint alleged a deprivation of their rights under ADEA and sought back wages, liquidated damages, reinstatement or front pay in lieu of reinstatement, and attorney's fees and costs, and demanded a trial by jury.

* * * The total settlement that Fox & Fox negotiated on behalf of the claimants amounted to $2,650,000, which was apportioned as follows pursuant to the contingent fee agreements:

Total recovery to class members	1,590,000
Total fee to Fox & Fox	1,060,000
Total settlement	2,650,000

Petitioner's allocated share of the gross settlement amount of $2,650,000 was $229,501.37. Of this amount, $32,476.61 was paid as lost wages by an APV check issued directly to petitioner. APV withheld applicable Federal and State employment taxes from this portion of the settlement; the actual net amount of the check to the order of petitioner was $21,246.20.

The portion of the settlement proceeds allocated to petitioner and not designated as lost wages was $197,024.76 * * *. After deducting its fee of $91,800.54 and crediting petitioner with the $500 "win or lose" retainer payment, Fox & Fox issued a check for $105,724.22 from the Fox & Fox trust account to petitioner.

* * *

OPINION

Petitioners concede that the proceeds from the settlement are includable in gross income except for the portion of the settlement used to pay Fox & Fox under the contingent fee agreement. Specifically, petitioners argue that they exercised insufficient control over the settlement proceeds used to pay Fox & Fox and should, therefore, not be taxed on amounts to which they had no "legal" right and could not, and did not, receive. Conversely, respondent argues that (1) the amount petitioners paid or incurred as attorney's fees must be included in petitioners' gross income and (2) the contingent fee is deductible as a miscellaneous itemized deduction, subject to the 2–percent floor under section 67 and the overall limitation under section 68 and also nondeductible in computing the alternative minimum tax (AMT) under section 56.

This controversy is driven by the substantial difference in the amount of tax burden that may result from the parties' approaches.[3] The difference, of course, is a consequence of the plain language of sections 56, 67, and 68, so the characterization of the attorney's fees as excludable or deductible becomes critical. There have been attempts to provide relief from the resulting tax burden by creative approaches, including attempts to modify long-standing tax principles. This Court believes that it is Congress' imposition of the AMT and limitations on personal itemized deductions that cause the tax burden here. We perceive dangers in the ad hoc modification of

3. Under respondent's position in this case, the settlement proceeds are included in petitioners' gross income in full, but the itemized deduction is subject to limitations and is not available in computing the alternative minimum tax (AMT). Under these circumstances, it is possible that the attorney's fees and tax burden could consume a substantial portion (possibly all) of the damages received by a taxpayer. It is noted, however, that if the recovery or income was received in a trade or business setting, the attorney's fees may be fully deductible in arriving at adjusted gross income, thereby obviating the perceived unfairness that may be occasioned in the circumstances we consider in this case. Commentators and courts have long observed this potential for unfairness in the operation of the AMT in this and other areas of adjustments and tax preference items. * * *

established tax law principles or doctrines to counteract hardship in specific cases, and, accordingly, we have not acquiesced in such approaches. * * * Despite this potential for unfairness, however, these policy issues are in the province of Congress, and we are not authorized to rewrite the statute. See, e.g., Badaracco v. Commissioner, 464 U.S. 386, 398, 78 L. Ed. 2d 549, 104 S. Ct. 756 (1984) * * *.

There is a split of authority among the Federal Courts of Appeals on this issue. The U.S. Court of Appeals for the Fifth Circuit reversed this Court and held that amounts awarded in Alabama litigation that were assigned and paid directly to cover attorney's fees pursuant to a contingent fee agreement are excludable from gross income. See Cotnam v. Commissioner, 263 F.2d 119 (5th Cir.1959), affg. in part and revg. in part 28 T.C. 947 (1957). In Cotnam, the taxpayer entered into a contingent fee agreement to pay her attorney 40 percent of any amount recovered on a claim prosecuted for the taxpayer's behalf. A judgment was obtained on the claim, and a check in the amount of the judgment was made jointly payable to the taxpayer and her attorney. The attorney retained his share of the proceeds and remitted the balance to the taxpayer. The Commissioner treated the total amount of the judgment as includable in the taxpayer's gross income and allowed the attorney's fees as an itemized deduction. This Court agreed with the Commissioner, holding that the taxpayer realized income in the full amount of the judgment, even though the attorney received 40 percent in accordance with the contingent fee agreement.

The U.S. Court of Appeals for the Fifth Circuit's reversal was based on two legal grounds. An opinion by Judge Wisdom on behalf of the panel reasoned that, under the Alabama attorney lien statute, an attorney has an equitable assignment or lien enabling the attorney to hold an equity interest in the cause of action to the extent of the contracted for fee. See 263 F.2d at 125. Under the Alabama statute, attorneys had the same right to enforce their lien as clients have or had for the amount due the clients. See id.

The other judges in Cotnam, Rives and Brown, in a separate opinion, stated that the claim involved was far from being perfected and that it was the attorney's efforts that perfected or converted the claim into a judgment. Judge Wisdom, in the second of his opinions, dissented, reasoning that the taxpayer had a right to the already-earned income and that it could not be assigned to the attorneys without tax consequence to the assignor. The Cotnam holding with respect to the Alabama attorney lien statutes has been distinguished by this Court from cases interpreting the statutes of numerous other states. Significantly, this Court has, for nearly 40 years, not followed Cotnam with respect to the analysis in the opinion of Judges Rives and Brown that the attorney's fee came within an exception to the assignment of income doctrine. See, e.g., Estate of Gadlow v. Commissioner, 50 T.C. 975, 979–980 (1968) * * *.

Addressing the assignment of income question in similar circumstances, the U.S. Court of Appeals for the Federal Circuit reached a result opposite from that reached in Cotnam. See Baylin v. United States, 43 F.3d 1451, 1454–1455 (Fed.Cir.1995). In Baylin, a tax matters partner entered into a contingent fee agreement with the partnership's attorney in a condemnation proceeding. When the litigants entered into a settlement, the attorney received his one-third contingency fee directly from the court in accordance with the fee agreement. On its tax return, the partnership reduced the amount realized from the condemnation by the amount of attorney's fees attributable to recovery of principal and deducted from ordinary income the attorney's fees attributed to the interest income portion of the settlement. The Government challenged this classification of the attorney's fees, determining that the attorney's fees constituted a capital expenditure and could, therefore, not reduce ordinary income.

The Court of Federal Claims agreed with the Government. On appeal, the taxpayer argued that the portion of the recovery used to pay attorney's fees was never a part of the partnership's gross income and should be excluded from gross income. The Federal Circuit, rejecting the taxpayer's argument, held that even though the partnership did not take possession of the funds that were paid to the attorney, it "received the benefit of those funds in that the funds served to discharge the obligation of the partnership owing to the attorney as a result of the attorney's efforts to increase the settlement amount." Id. at 1454. The Court of Appeals for the Federal Circuit sought to prohibit taxpayers in contingency fee cases from avoiding Federal income tax with "skillfully devised" fee agreements. See id.

* * *

In a recent holding, the U.S. Court of Appeals for the Sixth Circuit reached a result based on similar reasoning to that used in Cotnam. See Estate of Clarks v. United States, 202 F.3d 854 (6th Cir.2000). In Estate of Clarks, after a jury awarded the taxpayer personal injury damages and interest, the judgment debtor paid the taxpayer's lawyer the amount called for in the contingent fee agreement. Because the portion of the attorney's fee that was attributable to the recovery of taxable interest was paid directly to the attorney, the taxpayer excluded that amount from gross income on the estate's Federal income tax return. The Commissioner determined that the portion of the attorney's fees attributable to interest was deductible as a miscellaneous itemized deduction and was not excludable from gross income. The taxpayer paid the deficiency and sued for a refund in Federal District Court.

The District Court granted summary judgment in favor of the Government. The U.S. Court of Appeals for the Sixth Circuit reversed, employing reasoning similar to that used in Cotnam. The Court of Appeals held that, under Michigan law, the taxpayer's contingent fee agreement with the lawyer operated as a lien on the portion of the judgment to be recovered and transferred ownership of that portion of the judgment to the attorney.

The court seemed to place greater emphasis on the fact that the taxpayer's claim was speculative and dependent upon the services of counsel when it was assigned. In that respect, the court held that the assignment was no different from a joint venture between the taxpayer and the attorney. The court explained that this case was distinguishable from other assignment of income cases in that there was "no vested interest, only a hope to receive money from the lawyer's efforts and the client's right, a right yet to be determined by judge and jury." Id. at 857. The court stated:

> Here the client as assignor has transferred some of the trees in his orchard, not merely the fruit from the trees. The lawyer has become a tenant in common of the orchard owner and must cultivate and care for and harvest the fruit of the entire tract. Here the lawyer's income is the result of his own personal skill and judgment, not the skill or largess of a family member who wants to split his income to avoid taxation. The income should be charged to the one who earned it and received it, not as under the government's theory of the case, to one who neither received it nor earned it. The situation is no different from the transfer of a one-third interest in real estate that is thereafter leased to a tenant. [Id. at 858.][4]

This Court has, for an extended period of time, held the view that taxable recoveries in lawsuits are gross income in their entirety to the party-client and that associated legal fees—contingent or otherwise—are to be treated as deductions. See Bagley v. Commissioner, 105 T.C. 396, 418–419 (1995), affd. 121 F.3d 393, 395–396 (8th Cir.1997); O'Brien v. Commissioner, 38 T.C. 707, 712 (1962), affd. per curiam 319 F.2d 532 (3d Cir.1963); Benci–Woodward v. Commissioner, T.C. Memo 1998–395, on appeal (9th Cir., Feb. 2, 1999). In O'Brien, we held that "even if the taxpayer had made an irrevocable assignment of a portion of his future recovery to his attorney to such an extent that he never thereafter became entitled thereto even for a split second, it would still be gross income to him under" assignment of income principles. * * *. "Although there may be considerable equity to the taxpayer's position, that is not the way the statute is written." * * * In reaching this conclusion, we rejected the distinction made in Cotnam v. Commissioner, supra, with respect to the Alabama attorney's lien statute, stating that it is "doubtful that the Internal Revenue Code was intended to turn upon such refinements." * * * Numerous decisions of this Court have reached the same result as O'Brien by distinguishing other States' attorney's lien statutes from the Alabama statute considered in Cotnam. * * *

After further reflection on Cotnam and now Estate of Clarks v. United States, supra, we continue to adhere to our holding in O'Brien that contingent fee agreements, such as the one we consider here, come within

4. The Court of Appeals' analogy is, to some extent, inapposite because the transfer of trees in and of itself could be consideration in kind and result in gains to the taxpayer. More significantly, if the trees are analogous to the taxpayer's chose in action or compensatory rights, then the transfer represents a classic anticipatory assignment of income.

the ambit of the assignment of income doctrine and do not serve, for purposes of Federal taxation, to exclude the fee from the assignor's gross income. We also decline to decide this case based on the possible effect of various States' attorney's lien statutes.[5]

Section 61(a) provides that "gross income means all income from whatever source derived," and typically, all gains are taxed unless specifically excluded. * * * We can identify no specific exclusion from gross income for the payment made to Fox & Fox. While it is true that petitioner did not physically receive the portion of the settlement proceeds used to pay the attorney's fees, he did receive the full benefit of those funds in the form of payment for the services required to obtain the settlement. At the time that petitioner entered into the contingent fee agreement, he had already been discriminated against in the form of his wrongful termination from employment. In other words, petitioner was owed damages, and the attorney was willing to enter into a contingent fee agreement to recover the damages owed to petitioner. Therefore, petitioner must recognize as income the amount of the judgment.

In coming to this conclusion, we reject the significance placed by the U.S. Court of Appeals for the Sixth Circuit on the speculative nature of the claim and/or that the claim was dependent upon the assistance of counsel. Despite characterizing petitioner's right to recovery as speculative, his cause of action had value in the very beginning; otherwise, it is unlikely that Fox & Fox would have agreed to represent petitioner on a contingent basis. We find no meaningful distinction in the fact that the assistance of counsel was necessary to pursue the claim. Attorney's fees, contingent or otherwise, are merely a cost of litigation in pursuing a client's personal rights. Attorneys represent the interests of clients in a fiduciary capacity. It is difficult, in theory or fact, to convert that relationship into a joint venture or partnership. The entire ADEA award was "earned" by and owed to petitioner, and his attorney merely provided a service and assisted in realizing the value already inherent in the cause of action.

An anticipatory assignment of the proceeds of a cause of action does not allow a taxpayer to avoid the inclusion of income for the amount assigned. A taxpayer who enters into an agreement for the rendering of services that assists in the recovery from a third party must include the amount recovered (compensation) in gross income, irrespective of whether it is received by the taxpayer. * * * This Court, relying on Lucas v. Earl, 281 U.S. 111, 74 L. Ed. 731, 50 S. Ct. 241 (1930), has consistently held that a taxpayer cannot avoid taxation on his income by an anticipatory assignment of that income to another. * * * Thus, any anticipatory assignment

5. With the exception of situations where, under our holding in Golsen v. Commissioner, 54 T.C. 742, 756–757 (1970), affd. 445 F.2d 985 (10th Cir.1971), we feel compelled to follow the holding of a Court of Appeals, we have consistently held that attorney's fees are not subtracted from taxpayers' gross income to arrive at adjusted gross income. * * *

by the taxpayer of the proceeds of the lawsuit must be included in the taxpayer's gross income.

We reject petitioner's contention that he had insufficient control over his cause of action to be taxable on a recovery of a portion of the settlement proceeds that was diverted to or paid to Fox & Fox under the contingent fee agreement. There is no evidence supporting petitioner's contention that he had no control over his claim [under Wisconsin law]. * * *

Although petitioner may have entrusted Fox & Fox with the details of his litigation, ultimate control was not relinquished. If petitioner wanted to proceed without Fox & Fox, he could have obtained new representation.

The assignment of income doctrine was originated by the Supreme Court and has evolved over the past 70 years. See Helvering v. Eubank, 311 U.S. 122, 85 L. Ed. 81, 61 S. Ct. 149 (1940); Helvering v. Horst, 311 U.S. 112, 85 L. Ed. 75, 61 S. Ct. 144 (1940); Lucas v. Earl, supra. Although legislation may result in anomalous or inequitable results with respect to particular taxpayers, we are not in a position to address those policy questions. So, for example, if the AMT computation effectively renders de minimis a taxpayer's recovery due to the nondeductibility of the attorney's fees, we should not be tempted to modify established assignment of income principles to remedy the situation. That could result in a certain class of taxpayer's (those who receive reportable income from judgments) being treated differently from all other taxpayers who are subject to the AMT. These are matters within Congress' authority to decide. Congress, not the Courts, is the final arbiter of how the tax burden is to be borne by taxpayers.

Even if we were willing to follow the Cotnam and/or Estate of Clarks "attorney's lien" rationale, our analysis of the Wisconsin statutes and case law would not result in excluding the attorney's fee from petitioners' gross income here. * * *

We conclude that petitioner's award, undiminished by the amount that he paid to Fox & Fox, is includable in his 1993 gross income. The amount paid to Fox & Fox is deductible subject to certain statutory limitations as determined by respondent. We have also considered petitioners' remaining arguments and, to the extent not mentioned herein, find them to be without merit. To reflect the foregoing,

* * *

Reviewed by the Court.

[Seven other judges joined in the majority opinion and five judges dissented].

Page 69:

At the end of the carryover paragraph, insert:

As discussed in the *Kenseth* opinion, there have been a large number of cases in recent years dealing with the question of whether the portion of a taxable damage award retained by the taxpayer-plaintiff's attorney as a contingent fee is includable in the taxpayer's gross income, with a possible deduction for the payment (as discussed in Chapter 19 of the text) or whether only the net amount received by the taxpayer-plaintiff is includable in gross income. Although courts have tended to discuss the question in terms of property rights/joint venture analysis versus an assignment of income analysis, the question also can be viewed as analogous to the issue raised by *Old Colony Trust Co.*, text, page 66. Only the Sixth Circuit, in Estate of Clarks v. United States, 202 F.3d 854 (6th Cir.2000), and the Fifth Circuit in *Cotnam*, text, page 68, both of which are discussed in *Kenseth*, have held that the taxpayer-plaintiff may exclude from gross income the portion of the otherwise taxable damage award retained by the taxpayer's lawyer as a contingent fee. After *Kenseth* was decided, the Fifth Circuit reaffirmed and broadened its holding in *Cotnam* by holding in Srivastava v. Commissioner, 220 F.3d 353 (5th Cir.2000), that contingent fees retained by the taxpayer-plaintiff's attorney are excludable from the taxpayer's gross income in all cases, without regard to the particularities of the relevant state attorney's lien law. The taxpayer in *Srivastava* lived in Texas, and the Fifth Circuit held that *Cotnam* could not be distinguished because there is no difference in the "economic reality facing the taxpayer-plaintiff" between Alabama and Texas attorney's liens. Any distinction between them would not affect the analysis under the anticipatory assignment of income doctrine. The court acknowledged, however, that if the case had been before it as a matter of fist impression, it would have held that the attorney's fees were includable in the taxpayer's gross income under the anticipatory assignment of income doctrine, as are non-contingent attorney's fees. Nevertheless, the court declined to reconsider its decision in *Cotnam*. Like the Tax Court in *Kenseth* and the Federal Circuit in *Baylin*, text, page 68, the Courts of Appeals for the First, Fourth, Seventh, Eighth, Ninth, and Tenth Circuits all have held that the attorney's fees are includable in the plaintiff-taxpayer's gross income. See Alexander v. IRS, 72 F.3d 938 (1st Cir.1995); Young v. Commissioner, 240 F.3d 369 (4th Cir. 2001); Kenseth v. Commissioner, 259 F.3d 881 (7th Cir.2001); Bagley v. Commissioner, 121 F.3d 393 (8th Cir.1997); Coady v. Commissioner, 213 F.3d 1187 (9th Cir.2000); Benci–Woodward v. Commissioner, 219 F.3d 941 (9th Cir.2000); Hukkanen–Campbell v. Commissioner, 274 F.3d 1312 (10th Cir.2001). The Eleventh Circuit has applied the *Golsen* rule, text page 23, to follow *Cotnam* in cases involving taxpayers from Alabama,[1] see Davis v. Commissioner, 210 F.3d 1346 (11th Cir.2000) (per curiam); Foster v. United States, 249 F.3d 1275 (11th Cir.2001), but has not otherwise addressed the issue.

1. Under Bonner v. City of Prichard, Alabama, 661 F.2d 1206 (11th Cir.1981), Fifth Circuit decisions rendered before the Eleventh Circuit was created, by carving Alabama, Florida, and Georgia out of the old Fifth Circuit, are binding precedent in the Eleventh Circuit.

In Sinyard v. Commissioner, 268 F.3d 756 (9th Cir.2001), the taxpayer was required to include in gross income the portion of the settlement of a suit under the Age Discrimination in Employment Act (ADEA) that was paid directly to the attorneys as their fee pursuant to the settlement agreement. This result was reached even though if the suit gone to trial and the taxpayer won, under the ADEA the defendant would have been statutorily liable for the taxpayer-plaintiff's attorneys' fees in addition to compensatory damages to the plaintiff. Judge McKeown, who wrote the Ninth Circuit's opinion in *Benci–Woodward*, supra, which held that contingent attorneys' fees are included in the successful plaintiff's gross income, dissented. The dissent reasoned that *Sinyard* was distinguishable from *Benci-Woodward* and *Old Colony Trust*, text, page 66, because by virtue of the ADEA statutory attorney's fees provisions, contingent attorney's fees incurred in an ADEA suit never become a debt of the taxpayer and the payment thus was not an indirect payment of a damage award or settlement to the taxpayer.

Notwithstanding this conflict among the Circuit Courts of Appeals, the Supreme Court has declined to grant certiorari to consider the issue. Coady v. Commissioner, supra, cert. denied, 532 U.S. 972 (2001); Hukkanen–Campbell v. Commissioner, 535 U.S. 1056, 122 S.Ct. 1915 (2002).

Section 3. Noncash Benefits

Page 77:

After the carryover paragraph, insert:

Every major airline offers a "frequent flyer program" under which customers accumulate points or "miles" toward a "free" airline trip. How should the receipt of these points or airplane tickets be treated? The frequent flyer awards can be viewed as a "price rebate," reflecting a market bargain purchase price accorded by the airlines to frequent customers. This theory presents no problems if the purchased tickets that generated award trips involved personal travel. In practice, however, most frequent flyer points are generated by business travel for which the traveler's employer pays, and which is not included in the traveler's gross income, or which is claimed as a deduction by a self employed traveler, while a large number of award trips are used for personal purposes. In Announcement 2002–18, 2002–10 I.R.B. 621, the Service announced that as a matter of administrative policy, "Consistent with prior practice, the IRS will not assert that any taxpayer has understated his federal tax liability by reason of the receipt or personal use of frequent flyer miles or other in-kind promotional benefits attributable to the taxpayer's business or official travel." The Service cautioned, however, that this safe harbor is inapplicable to benefits that are converted to cash, to compensation paid in the form of benefits, or where these benefits "are used for tax avoidance purposes."

CHAPTER 3

EMPLOYEE FRINGE BENEFITS

SECTION 1. EXCLUSION BASED ON TAX POLICY AND ADMINISTRATIVE CONVENIENCE

Page 100:

After the second full paragraph, insert:

American Airlines, Inc. v. United States, 204 F.3d 1103 (Fed.Cir.2000), held that $50 American Express vouchers charged to the employer's account and provided to employees for their use at restaurants while traveling, but the use of which as a practical matter was not restricted, were cash equivalents that were not excludable as *de minimis* fringe benefits.

Page 103:

Omit the second sentence of the carryover paragraph and insert:

As amended in 1998, § 132(f) limits the aggregate exclusion to $175 per month for qualified parking and $65 per month in the aggregate ($100 after 2001) for transit passes and qualified highway vehicle use. These amounts are indexed for inflation.

At the end of the carryover paragraph, insert:

Treas. Reg. § 1.132–9 provides in a Question and Answer format detailed rules regarding the scope of qualified transportation fringe benefits.

After the first full paragraph, insert:

E1. QUALIFIED RETIREMENT PLANNING SERVICES

Section 132(a)(7), added by the 2001 Act, excludes from gross income the value of "qualified retirement planning services." Qualified retirement planning services are defined in § 132(m) as retirement planning advice or information provided to an employee and his spouse by an employer maintaining a qualified pension plan. Qualified advice is not limited to matters related to the qualified pension plan on which eligibility is based; it may extend to retirement income planning generally and how the employer's plan fits into the employee's overall retirement income planning. Section 132(m) does not, however, extend to the value of tax preparation, accounting, legal and brokerage services related to retirement planning. The exclusion under § 132(a)(7) is subject to a nondiscrimination rule making it available to highly compensated employees "only if such services are available on substantially the same terms to each member of the group of employees normally provided education and information regarding the employer's qualified employer plan." The legislative history indicates that this standard should permit employers to limit certain types of advice to individuals nearing retirement.

Page 105:

At the end of the second full paragraph, insert:

In Announcement 99–77, 1999–2 C.B. 243, the IRS announced that in applying § 119(a)(1) and the regulations it "will not attempt to substitute its judgment for the business decisions of an employer as to what specific business policies and practices are best suited to addressing the employer's business concerns." It does, however, caution taxpayers that " 'it would not [be] enough for [an employer] to wave a "magic wand" and say it had a policy in order [for meals to qualify under § 119].' " The IRS "will consider whether the employer's policies are reasonably related to the needs of the employer's business (apart from a desire to provide additional compensation to its employees) and whether these policies are in fact followed in the actual conduct of the business." If reasonable procedures are adopted and applied, and they preclude employees from obtaining a meal away from the employer's business premises during a reasonable meal period, § 119 will apply. It appears from this statement that the IRS will not question an employer's judgment in prohibiting or restricting employees' ability to leave the business premises for meals, however unreasonable that judgment might be to outsiders, but it will demand that the employer actually prohibit or restrict employees from leaving the business premises for meals in order for § 119 to apply.

Page 105:

After the second full paragraph, insert:

Section 119(b)(4), added in 1998, provides that if more than one-half of the meals furnished to employees on an employer's business premises satisfy the "convenience of the employer test," then all meals furnished to all employees on those premises are deemed to have been provided for the convenience of the employer.

SECTION 2. EXCLUSIONS TO FURTHER SOCIAL POLICY GOALS

Page 109:

In the Code citations omit section "120(a)–(c)" and insert "section 129".

In the Regulations citations, insert:

Sections 1.105–1, –2; 1.106–1.

Page 110:

At the end of the carryover paragraph, insert:

Tuka v. Commissioner, 120 T.C. 1 (2003) (disability payments, based on age, years of service, and salary, received from an employer sponsored plan were not exempt under § 104(a)(3) because exemption for disability benefits applies only if contributions to the accident and health plan were includible in the employee's gross income; that the plan might have been funded by wage savings to the employer resulting from collective bargaining with the union did not make it an employee contribution plan).

Page 112:

At the end of the second full paragraph, insert:

The 2001 Act made § 127 a "permanent" provision and extended it to include graduate education for employees, as well as undergraduate education. Like all of the amendments in the 2001 Act, however, these changes sunset on December 31, 2010.

Page 113:

After the carryover paragraph, insert:

The 2001 Act made § 137 a "permanent" provision, subject to sunset in 2011 like all of the other provisions of the 2001 Act. In addition, the 2001 Act increased the ceiling on the exclusion to $10,000, subject to an annual inflation adjustment. The 2001 Act changed the phase-out rule by amending § 137 to begin the phase-out of the adoption expense exclusion when the employee's adjusted gross income exceeds $150,000, subject to an annual inflation adjustment. Apart from the inflation adjustment, it is completely phased out when the employee's adjusted gross income exceeds $190,000.

CHAPTER 4

WINDFALLS, GIFTS, INHERITANCES, AND SIMILAR ITEMS

SECTION 2. GIFTS AND INHERITANCES

B. THE MEANING OF "GIFT" OR "INHERITANCE"

Page 132:

After the second full paragraph, insert:

Rev. Rul. 2003–12, 2003–3 I.R.B. 283, held that amounts received by an individual from an employer to reimburse the individual for necessary medical, temporary housing, or transportation expenses incurred as a result of a flood are not excludable as a gift under § 102, but are excluded from gross income as qualified disaster relief under § 139 if the flood was a Presidentially declared disaster; similar amounts received from a charity, however, are excluded under § 102, as are similar amounts received from a state agency under the administratively developed general welfare exclusion, discussed at text page 152.

SECTION 3. LIFE INSURANCE DEATH BENEFITS

Page 138:

In the first line of the first full paragraph change the citation from "Rev. Rul. 65–67" to "Rev. Rul. 65–57."

SECTION 5. SCHOLARSHIPS

Page 148:

After the carryover paragraph, insert:

The 2001 Act amended § 117(c) to provide tax-exempt scholarship treatment to grants under the National Health Services Corps Scholarship Program and the Armed Forces Health Professions Scholarship and Financial Assistance Program without regard to any service obligation imposed on the scholarship recipient.

SECTION 6. GOVERNMENTAL SUBSIDIES AND RELATED ITEMS

B. SOCIAL WELFARE PAYMENTS

Page 156:

After the fourth full paragraph, insert:

Applying principles similar to those applied in Rev. Rul. 75–246, text, page 152, in Notice 99–3, 1999–1 C.B. 271, the Service ruled that because the right to payments received under Temporary Assistance for Needy Families (TANF), which replaced AFDC in 1996, sometimes is conditioned upon the recipient engaging in work activities, the payments received under TANF may be includable in gross income as compensation for services or excludable as social welfare payments, depending on the facts and circumstances of the particular taxpayer's right to receive payments under the program.

Page 157:

In second to the last line of the first full paragraph, change "$3,500" to "$4,500" and "$4,000" to "$6,000."

CHAPTER 5

Loans and Other Receipts Balanced by Offsetting Obligations

Section 1. Loans

Page 164:

After the principal case, Milenbach v. Commissioner, insert:

Milenbach v. Commissioner

United States Court of Appeals, Ninth Circuit, 2003.
318 F.3d 924.

■ Tashima, Circuit Judge.

* * *

I. THE LAMCC PAYMENTS

A. Background

* * *

The Tax Court held that the "loan" payments from the LAMCC were includable in the Raiders' income in the years in which they were received. * * * It held that the obligation to construct the suites was illusory and, therefore, the LAMCC payments did not qualify as loans for tax purposes because the Raiders "controlled whether or not repayment of the $6.7 million would be triggered." * * *

B. Analysis

* * *

A loan is generally not taxable income because the receipt of the loan is offset by the obligation to repay the loan. Comm'r v. Tufts, 461 U.S. 300, 307 * * * (1983). For this rule to apply, however, the loan must be an "existing, unconditional, and legally enforceable obligation for the payment of a principal sum." Noguchi v. Comm'r, 992 F.2d 226, 227(9th Cir.1993); * * *

Whether a transaction is a loan for federal income tax purposes is ultimately a question of federal law. See Helvering v. Stuart, 317 U.S. 154, 162 * * * (1942) ("Once rights are obtained by local law, whatever they may be called, these rights are subject to the federal definition of taxability."). Initially, however, state law determines the rights and obligations of the parties to a transaction. * * * But once an obligation is created by local law, it is subject to the federal definition of taxability. * * * Here, the dispositive question is whether the LAMCC Agreement was sufficient, under California law, to subject the Raiders to a non-illusory and enforceable obligation to repay the LAMCC advances. If the Raiders were subject to an "existing, unconditional, and legally enforceable obligation" to repay the LAMCC advances, the advances are properly treated as loans for federal income tax purposes. * * *

Contrary to the Tax Court's conclusion, the Raiders' broad discretion in the timing of the construction of the suites did not make the contract illusory. Under California law, an obligation under a contract is not illusory if the obligated party's discretion must be exercised with reasonableness or good faith. See Storek & Storek, Inc. v. Citicorp Real Estate, Inc., 100 Cal.App.4th 44, 122 Cal.Rptr.2d 267, 281 (2002) (holding that a promise to pay only if satisfied is not illusory if the ability to claim dissatisfaction is limited by the standard of reasonableness). * * *

Here, the Raiders were required to exercise their discretion reasonably and nothing in the LAMCC Agreement indicates that construction of the suites was optional. Both the 1982 MOA and the Lease state that the suites "shall be" constructed and both require the Raiders to use their "reasonable" discretion in deciding the exact timing in the construction of the suites. The Lease also required the Raiders to use their "best efforts" both to construct the suites as soon as possible and to operate them in such a way as to maximize the profits to be derived from them. At no point were the Raiders free to ignore their obligation to construct the suites. They could only delay the construction for a reasonable time and were required to use their best efforts to complete the suites and begin repayment of the loan. These limitations on the Raiders' discretion were sufficient to create a non-illusory obligation both to construct the suites and to repay the loan that would have been enforceable under California law. The fact that the obligations were later extinguished by the settlement of the 1987 lawsuit does not indicate that the obligation was illusory at the time the contract was made. Accordingly, we conclude that the Tax Court erred in holding that the LAMCC Agreement was illusory.

CHAPTER 6

INCOME FROM DEALINGS IN PROPERTY

SECTION 3. DETERMINING THE AMOUNT OF GAIN

A. SALES OF PROPERTY AND TRANSFERS OF PROPERTY IN SATISFACTION OF A CLAIM

Page 221:

After the first full paragraph, insert:

In Gladden v. Commissioner, 262 F.3d 851 (9th Cir.2001), the taxpayer, who was engaged in a farming business, received from the Department of the Interior payments in exchange for surrender of his rights to a water allotment, which were appurtenant to the land. The Tax Court held that the taxpayer, who acquired the land in 1976 and acquired the appurtenant water rights in 1983, could not allocate any portion of the basis of the land to the water rights under Treas. Reg. § 1.61–6(a) because the water rights were not vested at the time the land was purchased. The Court of Appeals reversed. It rejected the taxpayer's argument that it should follow *Inaja Land Co.*, text, page 219, to permit the taxpayer simply to apply the amount received against his basis in the land. The court reasoned that if there had not been an expectation of a subsequent allocation of water rights to the land at the time of its purchase, none of the cost of the land would have been apportionable to the water rights. But because there had been an expectation of a subsequent allocation of water rights to the land at the time of its purchase, the land could have commanded a premium that properly should have been allocated to the basis of the water rights. The Court of Appeals remanded the case for a factual determination of whether a portion of the cost of the land was a premium paid for the water rights later acquired, or whether it is "impracticable or impossible" to determine what that premium may have been.

CHAPTER 7

DAMAGE AWARDS AND SETTLEMENTS AND INSURANCE RECOVERIES

SECTION 2. DAMAGE AWARDS FOR PERSONAL INJURY

Page 240:

In the first line of the first full paragraph, change the citation from "§ 104(b)(2)" to "§ 104(a)(2)."

Page 241:

After the first paragraph, insert:

In Prasil v. Commissioner, T.C. Memo 2003–100, the taxpayer received $7,650 to settle a sex discrimination claim against her employer. The court held that § 104(a)(2) did not exclude the payment from gross income. The record was devoid of any evidence to corroborate the taxpayer's "own self-serving testimony * * * that [the employer's] sex discrimination caused a physical injury to or the physical sickness of Mrs. Prasil." Furthermore, the settlement agreement referred only to the sex discrimination claim and "did not specifically carve out any portion of the settlement payment as a settlement on account of personal physical injury or physical sickness, let alone make reference to a physical injury or a physical sickness * * *."

CHAPTER 9

THE RELATIONSHIP OF BASIS TO INCOME RECOGNITION

SECTION 1. GRATUITOUS TRANSFERS

B. TRANSFERS AT DEATH: FAIR MARKET VALUE BASIS

Page 264:

After the last paragraph, insert:

E. MODIFIED CARRYOVER BASIS AT DEATH STARTING IN 2010

The 2001 Act repealed the estate tax as of January 1, 2010. I.R.C. § 2210. In this context, Congress also enacted § 1022, which will replace § 1014 on January 1, 2010. Section 1022(a) sets forth a "general rule" under which the basis of inherited property would be the lesser of the decedent's adjusted basis for the property or the fair market value of the property on the decedent's date of death. This general rule, however, is limited by an exception in § 1022(b)(1)(A) that provides a basis increase of up to $1,300,000.[1] Assume, for example, that a parent died and the parent's sole child inherited Blackacre, which was the parent's only item of property, and on the date of the parent's death, Blackacre had an adjusted basis to parent of $200,000. If the fair market value of Blackacre were $1,100,000, the child would have an adjusted basis of $1,100,000 in Blackacre. See I.R.C. 1022(d)(2), limiting the resulting basis to the property's fair market value. If the fair market value of Blackacre were $1,700,000, the child would have an adjusted basis of only $1,500,000 in Blackacre because the basis can be increased by only $1,300,000. Section 1022(c) provides a special rule providing an additional basis increase of up to $3,000,000 for property inherited by a surviving spouse of the decedent. This greater spousal basis increase is not available for most terminable interests, although it is available for property passing to certain types of trusts for the benefit of a surviving spouse. See I.R.C. § 1022(c)(3)–(5). Section 1022(d)(4) provides that both the $1,300,000 and $3,000,000 basis increase allowances are subject to adjustment for inflation beginning in 2011, which is a year after the changes in the 2001 Act sunset.

1. The aggregate basis increase is increased by the amount by which the basis of any property exceeds the property's fair market value if a loss would have been allowed under § 165 if the decedent had sold the property, I.R.C. § 1022(b)(2)(C), even though a particular item of property may not take a basis in the hands of the heir that exceeds its fair market value.

If a husband and wife own property as joint tenants, the deceased spouse is treated as owning fifty-percent of the property immediately before his or her death. I.R.C. § 1022(d)(1)(B). In the case of other joint tenancies, the decedent is treated as owning a percentage of the property proportionate to the consideration provided to acquire and improve the property. If a husband and wife own property as community property, the deceased spouse is treated as owning all of the property. I.R.C. § 1022(d)(1)(C). This special rule is analogous to § 1014(b)(6) and permits the basis increase to apply to the entire property rather than only to one-half of the surviving spouse's interest as is the case in common law states.

The basic $1,300,000 basis increase and the special $3,000,000 spousal basis increase can be pyramided. A surviving spouse who is the sole heir or legatee of the decedent thus can obtain an aggregate basis increase of $4,300,000. See I.R.C. § 1022(c)(1). Alternatively, another heir can obtain a basis increase of $1,300,000 while the spouse obtains a basis increase of up to $3,000,000. Assume for example, that the decedent dies owning Blackacre and Whiteacre and bequeaths Blackacre to a surviving spouse and Whiteacre to a child. Blackacre had an adjusted basis in the decedent's hands of $500,000 and a fair market value at decedent's death of $3,400,000; it is appreciated by $2,900,000. Whiteacre had an adjusted basis in the decedent's hands of $200,000 and a fair market value at decedent's death of $1,600,000; it is appreciated by $1,400,000. The spouse would take a $3,400,000 basis in Blackacre and the child would take a $1,500,000 basis in Whiteacre. The unusable $100,000 of the spousal basis increase can not be transferred to Whiteacre. But if Blackacre had a fair market value of $3,700,000 and Whiteacre had a fair market value of $1,400,000, the unused $100,000 of the $1,300,000 basis increase that remained after Whiteacre's basis had been increased to $1,400,000, its fair market value, can be allocated to Blackacre, to bring its basis up to $3,600,000. See I.R.C. § 1022(c)(1).

If the aggregate appreciation in all of a decedent's assets does not exceed the applicable limit, then no problem of apportioning the basis increase among assets arises. But if the aggregate appreciation in the decedent's assets exceeds the applicable limit, then the basis increase must be apportioned. Section 1022(c) provides that the decedent's executor shall allocate the basis increase, but provides no rules for how to allocate it. Assume for example, that the decedent dies owning Blackacre and Whiteacre and bequeaths Blackacre to child A and Whiteacre to child B. Blackacre had an adjusted basis in the decedent's hands of $300,000 and a fair market value at decedent's death of $1,600,000; it is appreciated by $1,300,000. Whiteacre had an adjusted basis in the decedent's hands of $200,000 and a fair market value at decedent's death of $850,000; it is appreciated by $650,000. The statute is silent regrading whether the $1,300,000 basis increase is to be apportioned two-thirds ($866,667) to Blackacre and one-third ($433,333) to Whiteacre or whether, the executor is permitted—at least under the Internal Revenue Code, even if possibly not under state law—to allocate the basis increase all to Blackacre, or alternatively in any other manner, for example, $650,000 to each property. This can an important question even if a single heir or legatee acquires all of the decedent's property. Generally speaking, it always will be advantageous for tax purpose to skew the basis increase allocation, if permissible (1) to depreciable property, e.g., building, as opposed to nondepreciable property, e.g., land, (2) to property likely to be sold sooner rather than property that will be sold later or which will be held indefinitely, and (3) to property that would result in ordinary income treatment upon sale rather than long-term capital gain. Luckily, the Treasury Department has eight years to work on the regulations before the rules come into effect!

To forestall a morbid tax avoidance planning device, § 1022(d)(1)(C) denies the basis increase with respect to any property received by the decedent by gift, except from the decedent's spouse, within three years prior to death. Absent this rule, a child could make a gift of highly appreciated property to a terminally ill parent shortly before the parent's death with an arrangement that the parent would bequeath the property to the child. Section 1014(e) currently provides an analogous rule if a decedent acquires property by gift within one year of death

Like all of the other amendments to the Code in the 2001 Act, however, § 1022 sunsets on December 31, 2010. Thus, absent further congressional action, the modified carryover basis rules of § 1022 will be in effect only for 2010, and on January 1, 2011, § 1014 will be become effective once again.

CHAPTER 10

INCOME FROM DISCHARGE OF INDEBTEDNESS

SECTION 1. IDENTIFYING THE GAIN

Page 284:

After the second full paragraph, insert:

In Jelle v. Commissioner, 116 T.C. 63 (2001), the taxpayer owed $269,828 to the Farmers Home Administration (FmHA) on a mortgage loan secured by the taxpayer's farm, which was appraised at a value of $92,057. The taxpayer paid the FmHA the $92,057 "net recovery value" of the loan in exchange for cancellation of the remaining $177,772 of the debt, but the cancellation was a subject to "net recovery buyout recapture agreement" under which the taxpayer agreed to repay *pro tanto* the amounts written off by the FmHA in the event that he disposed of the farm within a 10–year period for a price that exceeded the $92,057 net recovery value. The taxpayer argued that the debt had not been cancelled before the end of the 10–year period because the "net recovery buyout recapture agreement" was a continuing obligation. The Tax Court disagreed and held that the overall agreement resulted in immediate cancellation of indebtedness income of $177,772 because there was only "the mere chance of some future repayment." The recapture agreement was not a substitute for taxpayer's former obligation.

Page 285:

At the end of the fourth full paragraph, insert:

Although the insolvency exclusion originated as a judicial exception to the *Kirby Lumber Co.* principle, in Gitlitz v. Commissioner, 531 U.S. 206, 121 S.Ct. 701 (2001), the Supreme Court held that the enactment of § 108(e) has pre-empted the field. The statutory insolvency exception is exclusive, and prior judicial principles cannot be applied to expand or narrow the statutory rules.

The statutory insolvency exception was applied in Carlson v. Commissioner, 116 T.C. 87 (2001), in which the Tax Court held that the definition of "insolvent" in § 108(d)(3) requires that all of the taxpayer's assets, including assets exempt from the claims of creditors under state law, be included in determining whether the taxpayer's liabilities exceed his assets. The taxpayer had argued that assets exempt from creditors' claims under state law should be excluded from the calculation, thus making it easier for a taxpayer to demonstrate insolvency. The court rejected this argument. It compared the definition of "insolvent" under the Bankruptcy Code, 11 U.S.C. § 101(26), which expressly excludes exempt property from the calculation, with the definition under § 108(d)(3), which does not do so, and concluded that the difference was intentional. In using the different definition Congress intended that exempt assets are not to be excluded from the calculation in determining whether the taxpayer is insolvent for purposes of § 108.

Page 287:

At the end of the last paragraph, insert:

Preslar v. Commissioner, 167 F.3d 1323 (10th Cir.1999), held that the enactment of § 108(e)(5) preempted any preexisting "common law" purchase price adjustment exception. The exception applies only to indebtedness owed by the purchaser to the seller of property. Accordingly, the exception was not available where a bank financed the taxpayer's purchase of property from a third party and the bank subsequently agreed to reduce the amount of the debt.

Page 288:

After the last paragraph, insert:

In Friedland v. Commissioner, T.C. Memo. 2001–236, the taxpayer pledged appreciated stock in a closely held corporation to a bank to secure a debt that his adult son owed to the bank. When the son defaulted on the loan, the taxpayer's stock was transferred to the bank in satisfaction of the son's debt. The court held that the taxpayer did not recognize any gain because no amount was realized on the transfer. Citing Landreth v. Commissioner, 50 T.C. 803 (1968), holding that a guarantor does not realize discharge of indebtedness income when the debtor is discharged from a debt, the court held that Treas. Reg. § 1.1001–2(a)(1) treats as an amount realized only the amount of the taxpayer's own indebtedness that is discharged by the transfer of property—not the amount of indebtedness of a third party. In a guarantee situation, satisfaction of the debt obligation by a guarantor creates a debt from the original debtor to the guarantor. Thus, in *Friedland*, failure by the son to pay this debt to the father would produce either COD income or a nontaxable gift to the son.

SECTION 2. THE NATURE OF THE DEBT

Page 299:

After Zarin v. Commissioner, insert:

Preslar v. Commissioner

United States Court of Appeals, Tenth Circuit, 1999.
167 F.3d 1323.

■ BRISCOE, CIRCUIT JUDGE.

The Commissioner of Internal Revenue appeals the United States Tax Court's decision to redetermine the tax deficiency assessed against Layne and Sue Preslar for underpayment of 1989 federal income taxes. The Tax Court held the Preslars' settlement of a loan obligation for less than the face amount of the loan did not create taxable income because the contested liability/disputed debt exception to the general discharge-of-indebtedness income rule rendered the write-off nontaxable. We exercise jurisdiction pursuant to 26 U.S.C. § 7482(a)(1), and reverse and remand.

I.

Layne Preslar, a real estate agent of twenty-five years, commenced negotiations in 1983 to purchase a 2500–acre ranch near Cloudcroft, New Mexico. High Nogal Ranch, Inc., owned the ranch and was a debtor-in-possession in a Chapter 11 bankruptcy proceeding. Citizens State Bank of Carrizozo, Security Bank and Trust of Alamogordo, and Moncor Bank held mortgages in the ranch. Moncor Bank, which had been experiencing serious financial difficulties and whose interest was subordinate to the other banks, took the lead in assisting in negotiations between High Nogal and Preslar. * * *

On July 12, 1983, after six months of talks, Layne and Sue Preslar agreed to purchase the ranch for $1 million, with the sale to be financed by Moncor Bank. The agreement expressly referred to the fact that Moncor Bank was financing the purchase, but only the Preslars and the president of High Nogal signed the contract on September 1, 1983. The Preslars executed a $1 million promissory note in favor of Moncor Bank, secured by a mortgage on the ranch. The Preslars were to pay fourteen annual installments of $66,667, with interest at twelve percent per annum, with final payment due September 1, 1998. * * *

The Preslars intended to develop the ranch as a sportsman's resort. * * *

Moncor Bank permitted the Preslars to repay their loan by assigning the installment sales contracts of purchasers of cabin lots to Moncor Bank at a discount. There is no reference to this unique repayment arrangement in the loan documents. * * * When each cabin lot was sold, the Preslars assigned and physically transferred the written sales contract to Moncor Bank. In return, Moncor Bank credited the Preslars' debt obligation in an amount equal to 95 percent of the stated principal contract price, regardless of actual payments received from the purchaser. Moncor Bank received a security interest in each lot sold to protect its interests in the event a purchaser defaulted. Between September 1983 and August 1985, the Preslars sold nineteen cabin lots and had assigned most of the contracts to Moncor Bank prior to its declared insolvency. Moncor Bank had credited the Preslars' principal loan balance with approximately $200,000. Funds applied to interest are not included in this amount; thus, the aggregate amount of discounted installment contracts assigned to Moncor Bank exceeded $200,000.

In August 1985, Moncor Bank was declared insolvent and the Federal Deposit Insurance Corporation (FDIC) was appointed as receiver. The FDIC notified the Preslars of the insolvency and advised them to make all future payments on their loan to the FDIC. The FDIC refused to accept further assignments of sale contracts as repayment and ordered the Preslars to suspend sales of cabin lots. The Preslars complied with the suspension directive, but made no further payments on the loan.

The Preslars filed an action against the FDIC for breach of contract in September 1985, seeking an order requiring the FDIC to accept assignment of sales contracts as loan repayment. The parties settled the action in December 1988 after the FDIC agreed to accept $350,000 in full satisfaction of the Preslars' indebtedness. The Preslars borrowed the $350,000 from another bank and, after the funds were remitted to the FDIC, the original $1 million promissory note was marked "paid."

At the time of the settlement, the unpaid balance on the Preslars' loan was $799,463. The Preslars paid a total of $550,537 on the loan ($350,000 settlement plus $200,537 credited for assignment of sales contracts). Therefore, as a result of the settlement, the Preslars' outstanding debt obligation was reduced by $449,463 ($1 million less $550,537).

The Preslars did not include the $449,463 debt write-off as discharge-of-indebtedness income on their 1989 joint tax return. Rather, they opted to reduce their basis in the ranch by $430,000 pursuant to Internal Revenue Code § 108(e)(5), 26 U.S.C. § 108(e)(5). The Preslars' 1989 tax return was audited and they were assessed a deficiency because (1) they had realized $449,463 in discharge-of-indebtedness income, and (2) they were not eligible to treat such income as a purchase price adjustment under § 108(e)(5). * * *

The Preslars sought a redetermination of the deficiency in United States Tax Court, insisting they were free to treat their settlement with the FDIC as a purchase price adjustment pursuant to § 108(e)(5) and/or common law. They supported this theory in part by claiming the FDIC's refusal to honor their repayment agreement with Moncor Bank amounted to an infirmity relating back to the original sale, thereby negating the general prohibition against treating debt reductions as purchase price adjustments. * * * At no time, however, did the Preslars dispute their underlying liability on the $1 million note.

* * *

The Tax Court ruled in favor of the Preslars without addressing the purchase price adjustment issue. Instead, the court *sua sponte* invoked the contested liability doctrine and held the Preslars' unusual payment arrangement with Moncor Bank caused their liability for the full $1 million loan to be brought into question. The court determined the true amount of the Preslars' indebtedness was not firmly established until they settled with the FDIC; thus, no discharge-of-indebtedness income could have accrued to the Preslars as a result of the settlement. * * *

II.

* * *

Discharge-of-Indebtedness Income

* * *

This case centers around the Commissioner's determination of the Preslars' discharge-of-indebtedness income after they settled their loan obligation with the FDIC in December 1988. The concept of discharge-of-indebtedness income, first articulated in United States v. Kirby Lumber Co., 284 U.S. 1, 52 S.Ct. 4, 76 L.Ed. 131 (1931), and later codified in 26 U.S.C. § 61(a)(12), requires taxpayers who have incurred a financial obligation that is later discharged in whole or in part, to recognize as taxable income the extent of the reduction in the obligation. Two rationales have been identified for this rule:

> This rule is based on the premise that the taxpayer has an increase in wealth due to the reduction in valid claims against the taxpayer's assets. In the alternative it has been suggested that taxation is appropriate because the consideration received by a taxpayer in exchange for [his] indebtedness is not included in income when received because of the obligation to repay and the cancellation of that obligation removes the reason for the original exclusion.

2 Jacob Mertens, Jr., Mertens Law of Federal Income Taxation § 11.01 (1996). Loans ordinarily are not taxable because the borrower has assumed an obligation to repay the debt in full at some future date. * * * Discharge-of-indebtedness principles come into play, however, if that assumption of repayment proves erroneous. Otherwise, taxpayers could secure income with no resulting tax liability.

It is undisputed that the Preslars financed their purchase of the ranch in 1983 by executing a $1 million promissory note in favor of Moncor Bank. It is similarly uncontested that when the Preslars settled their lawsuit with the FDIC in 1988, thereby extinguishing all obligations arising from the 1983 loan, only $550,537 had been paid on the loan principal. Nevertheless, the Tax Court ruled the Preslars' underlying debt was disputed and fell within the judicially-created "contested liability" exception to discharge-of-indebtedness income.

Contested Liability/Disputed Debt Exception

The "contested liability" or, as it is occasionally known, "disputed debt" doctrine rests on the premise that if a taxpayer disputes the original amount of a debt in good faith, a subsequent settlement of that dispute is "treated as the amount of debt cognizable for tax purposes." Zarin v. Commissioner, 916 F.2d 110, 115 (3d Cir.1990). In other words, the "excess of the original debt over the amount determined to have been due" may be disregarded in calculating gross income. Id. The few decisions that have interpreted this doctrine have generated considerable controversy.

The origins of the contested liability doctrine can be traced to N. Sobel, Inc. v. Commissioner, 40 B.T.A. 1263, (1939) * * *. In that case, a New York corporation purchased 100 shares of a bank's stock and signed a $21,700 note as payment. When the note matured, the stock was worthless. The corporation sued the bank for rescission, insisting the loan contravened state law and the bank had failed to fulfill its promise to guarantee the corporation against loss. Shortly thereafter, the state superintendent of banks closed the bank because of insolvency and initiated a countersuit against the corporation for the amount of the note. The parties ultimately settled the consolidated proceedings with the corporation paying the superintendent $10,850 in return for discharge of the debt. The corporation then took a $10,850 deduction in the year of settlement. The Commissioner disallowed the deduction and assessed a $10,850 deficiency, representing the amount of the original loan over the settlement figure. The Board of Tax Appeals reversed the ruling and upheld the deduction, concluding the corporation's ownership of the shares and the degree of liability on the note were highly unclear. * * * The Board found the corporation's financial obligations could not be assessed definitively prior to resolution of its dispute with the superintendent and, since settlement compromised the parties' claims and precluded recognition of their legal rights, the existence and amount of the corporation liability were not fixed until the date of settlement. Thus, release of the note did not amount to a gain for the corporation.

In *Zarin*, the court embraced the reasoning of N. Sobel while reversing the Commissioner's recognition of discharge-of-indebtedness income. The state gaming commission identified *Zarin* as a compulsive gambler and ordered an Atlantic City casino to refrain from issuing him additional credit, but the casino ignored the commission. When Zarin's debt surpassed $3.4 million, the casino filed a state action to collect the funds. Zarin initially denied liability on the grounds the casino's claim was unenforceable under New Jersey law. The parties later settled the dispute for $500,000. After Zarin failed to account for the debt write-off on his tax return, the Commissioner assessed a deficiency for approximately $2.9 million, the amount by which Zarin's underlying debt exceeded his settlement with the casino. The Tax Court affirmed. However, a divided Third Circuit held Zarin had no discharge-of-indebtedness income because, inter alia, his transaction with the casino arose from a contested liability. * * * Citing no authority, the majority reasoned that "[w]hen a debt is unenforceable, it follows that the amount of the debt, and not just the liability thereon, is in dispute." * * * Therefore, the $500,000 settlement "fixed the amount of loss and the amount of debt cognizable for tax purposes." * * *

The problem with the Third Circuit's holding is it treats liquidated and unliquidated debts alike. The whole theory behind requiring that the amount of a debt be disputed before the contested liability exception can be triggered is that only in the context of disputed debts is the Internal Revenue Service (IRS) unaware of the exact consideration initially exchanged in a transaction. * * * The mere fact that a taxpayer challenges the enforceability of a debt in good faith does not necessarily mean he or she is shielded from discharge-of-indebtedness income upon resolution of the dispute. To implicate the contested liability doctrine, the original amount of the debt must be unliquidated. A total denial of liability is not a dispute touching upon the amount of the underlying debt. One commentator has observed:

> Enforceability of the debt * * * should not affect the tax treatment of the transaction. If the parties initially treated the transaction as a loan when the loan proceeds were received, thereby not declaring the receipt as income, then the transaction should be treated consistently when the loan is discharged and income should be declared in the amount of the discharge.

Gregory M. Giangiordano, Taxation—Discharge of Indebtedness Income—Zarin v. Commissioner, 64 Temp. L.Rev. 1189, 1202 n.88 (1991). A holding to the contrary would strain IRS treatment of unenforceable debts and, in large part, disavow the Supreme Court's mandate that the phrase "gross income" be interpreted as broadly as the Constitution permits. See Glenshaw Glass, 348 U.S. at 432 & n. 11, 75 S.Ct. 473.

This conclusion is underscored by the Supreme Court's holding in Tufts that a nonrecourse mortgage (i.e., taxpayer has no personal liability upon default) must be treated as an enforceable loan both when it is made and when it is discharged. 461 U.S. at 311–13, 103 S.Ct. 1826. The Court reasoned that because the indebtedness is treated as a true debt when it is incurred, it must be treated as a true debt when it is discharged, with all the attendant tax consequences. Id. at 309–10, 103 S.Ct. 1826. It seems evident from this ruling that if the distinction between the recourse and nonrecourse nature of a loan has no bearing on calculation of gross income, the enforceability of a debt should be of equally minimal importance. Of course, if the debt is unenforceable as a result of an infirmity at the time of its creation (e.g., fraud or misrepresentation), tax liability may be avoided through a purchase price reduction under 26 U.S.C. § 108(e)(5) or an "infirmity exception."

* * *

In this case, the Tax Court observed that "the unusual payment arrangement between [the Preslars] and Moncor Bank relating to the Bank loan casts significant doubt on [the Preslars'] liability for the total $1 million stated principal amount of the Bank loan." Tax Ct. Op. at 8. Accepting the Preslars' contention that their $1 million purchase price had been inflated and did not reflect the fair market value of the ranch, the Tax Court suggested the Preslars had agreed to the terms of the financing arrangement only after Moncor Bank assented to a favorable repayment scheme involving assignment of installment sales contracts. The court held when the FDIC refused to honor this payment arrangement, "a legitimate dispute arose regarding the nature and amount of [the Preslars'] liability on the Bank loan." Id. Only after the Preslars and the FDIC settled their subsequent lawsuit, the court reasoned, was the amount of liability on the loan finally established.

It is conceivable that two parties could negotiate a loan transaction in which the underlying amount of a debt is tied to the existence or nonexistence of some post-execution event. Indeed, the IRS has defined "indebtedness" as "an obligation, absolute and not contingent, to pay on demand or within a given time, in cash or another medium, a fixed amount." Treas. Reg. § 1.108(b)–1(c), 26 C.F.R. § 1.108(b)–1(c) (1998). Contrary to the Tax Court's representations, however, there is no evidence of such an agreement here.

The Preslars advanced no competent evidence to support their theory that their loan obligation was linked to the repayment scheme. * * * Neither the May 1984 letter from Moncor Bank to Layne Preslar nor the unsigned 1985 Dealer Agreement * * * contains any statement evincing an intent to link the underlying liability with the repayment scheme. * * * Preslar's own self-serving testimony regarding the intentions of the parties to the original loan agreement is not sufficient to support the Preslars' integrated transaction theory. * * *

* * *

Although ultimately irrelevant, the Preslars offered no evidence, other than Layne Preslar's self-serving testimony, that the fair market value of the ranch differed from their $1 million purchase price. * * * Moreover, even if the Preslars could demonstrate the property was worth less than the purchase price, they still could not invoke the contested liability doctrine in the absence of proof the loan they executed was tainted by fraud or material misrepresentations, because the underlying amount of their debt obligation remained liquidated. * * * There are no allegations of fraud or misrepresentation in this case.

Purchase Price Adjustment

Another method by which taxpayers can avoid discharge-of-indebtedness income is to classify their debt reductions as purchase price adjustments. This rule permits taxpayers to reflect their debt reduction by adjusting the basis of their property rather than recognizing an immediate gain as cancellation of indebtedness. Although this principle had been part of the common law for decades, Congress codified the rule as part of the Bankruptcy Tax Act of 1980, Pub.L. No. 96–589, § 2(a), 94 Stat. 3389, 3389–90 (1980) (codified at 26 U.S.C. § 108(e)(5)).

* * *

The Preslars cannot treat their settlement with the FDIC as a purchase price reduction. Section 108(e)(5) applies only to direct agreements between a purchaser and seller. S.Rep. No. 96–1035 at 16 (1980) * * *. "If the debt has been transferred by the seller to a third party (whether or not related to the seller), or if the property has been transferred by the buyer to a third party (whether or not related to the buyer)," the purchase price reduction exception is not available and normal discharge-of-indebtedness rules control. * * * Although Moncor Bank helped negotiate the terms of the sale, it did so only in its capacity as a mortgage holder. * * *

III.

We REVERSE the Tax Court's vacatur of the Commissioner's determination of tax deficiency and * * * REMAND the case with instructions to enter judgment in favor of the Commissioner.

CHAPTER 11

TAX EXPENDITURES

SECTION 3. EXCLUSION OF GAINS FROM THE SALE OF A PRINCIPAL RESIDENCE

Pages 331–332:

Replace the paragraph beginning on page 331 and carrying over to page 332 with the following:

The ownership requirement is somewhat similar to the ownership requirement of former §§ 121 and 1034. Thus, property sold by estates and trusts generally does not qualify for the exclusion.[1] Sales by an individual's bankruptcy trustee, however, do qualify for the § 121 exclusion. Treas. Reg. § 1.1398–3. In addition, the two-out-of-five-year rule permits the sale of a principal residence that was abandoned and converted to rental use not more than three years previously to qualify for the exclusion, as long as it was continuously owned and used as a principal residence for at least two years prior to its conversion to rental property.

Omit the second through fourth full paragraphs on page 332 and insert:

If either spouse owned the property and both spouses satisfy the two-out-of-five-years occupancy test, § 121(b)(2), as retroactively amended in 1998, permits an exclusion of up to $500,000 on a joint return, as long as neither spouse has claimed the benefit of a § 121 exclusion for another sale within the 24 months preceding the sale in question. If one spouse is not eligible for an exclusion, for example, because he or she did not meet the two-out-of-five-years use test or because of the one-sale-every-two-years limitation of § 121(b)(3), then under § 121(b)(2)(B), the ceiling on the exclusion on a joint return is computed as if the husband and wife were single, except that the ownership of one continues to be attributed to the other. Thus, for example, if one spouse fails the use test, the ceiling is only $250,000. Similarly if § 121(b)(2) does not apply because one spouse (but not the other) had sold another house within the prior two years and

1. The 2001 Act added § 121(d)(9), which will become effective in 2010, to permit an estate or an individual who inherits a decedent's principal residence to claim the § 121 exclusion. Like all of the provisions in the 2001 Act, however, § 121(d)(9) sunsets on December 31, 2010.

If the taxpayer's principal residence is held by a trust, the taxpayer is treated as the owner and the seller of the residence during the period that the taxpayer is treated as the owner of the trust or the portion of the trust that includes the residence under §§ 671 through 679. Treas. Reg. § 1.121–1(c)(3)(i).

claimed an exclusion under § 121 (and that spouse was not eligible for exclusion with a reduced ceiling under § 121(c)), then the exclusion ceiling on the joint return would be only the $250,000 attributable to the fully eligible spouse. Section 121(b)(2)(B) is also applicable when taxpayers marry and then sell one or both of the principal residences they previously occupied when they were single, capping the exclusion of gain on the sale of each such residence at $250,000.

Page 334:

Omit the text of Item "C. PARTIAL NONRECOGNITION" and in its place insert:

If a taxpayer fails to meet either the two year use and ownership requirements of § 121(a) or the once-every-two-years limitation of § 121(b)(3) *and* the sale is due to a change in the taxpayer's place of employment or health, § 121(c) provides for partial nonrecognition. Since both the use and ownership test and the once-every-two years limitation employ the same base, § 121(c) reduces the ceiling on the amount of excludable gain. When § 121(c) applies, the $250,000 or $500,000 ceiling in § 121(a) or (b) is reduced by multiplying it by a fraction, the numerator of which is the number of months the taxpayer owned and used as a principal residence the house that was sold and the denominator of which is 24. Assume, for example, a single taxpayer moved from Boston to San Francisco in connection with a change of employment, had owned and lived in the Boston residence for 18 months, and realized a $180,000 gain on the sale of the Boston residence. The ceiling on the excludable gain under § 121(a) would be reduced from $250,000 to $187,500 ($250,000 x 18/24), and the entire $180,000 gain would be excludable. But if the Boston home had been sold for a $240,000 profit, only $187,500 would be excludable and the remaining $52,500 of gain would be taxable.

Page 335:

After the first full paragraph, insert:

The regulations provide a nonexclusive list of factors relevant to identifying the taxpayer's principal residence. The factors include: the taxpayer's place of employment, the principal abode of the taxpayer's family, the address used for filing tax returns, the address for the taxpayer's driver's license, automobile registration and voter's registration, the taxpayer's mailing address for bills and correspondence, the location of the taxpayer's banks, and the location of the taxpayer's social clubs and place of worship. Treas. Reg. § 1.121–1(b)(2). These factors cannot be conclusive because they can produce inconsistent evidence. For example, a taxpayer may receive bills and subscriptions and join social clubs and places of worship at two distant residences, and might hold a driver's license with an address different than the one used for filing tax returns.

Treas. Reg. § 1.121–1(b)(2) provides in part that the property used by the taxpayer for a majority of the time during the year will be treated as the taxpayer's principal residence. In Guinan v. United States, 91 A.F.T.R.2d 2003–2174 (D.Ariz.2003), the court interpreted this provision to apply to the use of multiple residences during each taxable year of the relevant two out of five year period. The taxpayers in *Guinan* owned three residences—a residence in Wisconsin, which they sold, a residence in Georgia, and a residence in Arizona. During the five year period the taxpayers spent more time in the aggregate in the Wisconsin residence (847 days) than in either of the other two residences (563 days in the Georgia residence and 375 days in the Arizona residence), although the taxpayers combined use of the Georgia and Arizona residences was greater than their use of the Wisconsin residence. The taxpayers spent the majority of their time in the Wisconsin residence only in the first year of the five year period. The other factors listed in Treas. Reg. § 1.121–1(b)(2) did not support treating the Wisconsin residence as the taxpayers' principal residence—the taxpayers had Arizona and Georgia driver's licenses, but not Wisconsin licenses and filed Arizona and Georgia state income tax returns, but not Wisconsin returns. Thus, the Wisconsin residence was not the taxpayers' principal residence and the § 121 exclusion was not available.

SECTION 4. TAX DEFERRED AND TAX EXEMPT INVESTMENT ACCOUNTS

Page 336:

After the last paragraph, insert:

The 2001 Act amended § 219 to increase the ceiling on deductible contributions to an IRA account to $3,000 for 2002 through 2004, $4,000 for 2005 through 2007, and $5,000 for 2008 and thereafter. Beginning in 2008, the $5,000 ceiling will be adjusted annually for inflation. In addition, taxpayers age 50 and older may deduct an additional $500 of contributions for 2002 through 2005 and an additional $1,000 for 2006 and thereafter.

The concept of participation in a qualified pension plan for purposes of determining whether the phase-out rules apply is form driven. In Wade v. Commissioner, T.C. Memo. 2001–114, Mrs. Wade was a part-time community college teacher who was found to be an active participant in a qualified plan by virtue of an $84.89 mandatory contribution to a defined benefit plan in a year in which she accrued approximately 1/120th of the service required for benefits to vest. As a result both Mrs. and Mr. Wade, whose combined AGI was $77,000, were denied deductions for their $2,000 IRA contributions under the § 219(g) phase-out rule.

Page 338:

Omit the second sentence of the second full paragraph and insert:

Unlike the case with regular IRAs, taxpayers who participate in an employer maintained qualified pension plan may establish a Roth IRA, subject to the general limitations based on the taxpayer's modified adjusted gross income.

SECTION 5. TAX EXPENDITURES FOR EDUCATION

Page 343:

After the third full paragraph, insert:

The 2001 Act made a number of changes in the EIRA rules, which were renamed Coverdell education savings accounts (to honor a Republican senator who died in office during the term) that are effective beginning in 2002. First, the annual limit on contributions was increased from $500 to $2,000. Contributions can qualify for a year as long as they are made during the year or during the following year but before the due date of the tax return for the year to which the contribution relates. I.R.C. § 530(f). Second, the phase-out rules in § 530 (c) were modified to provide a phase-out range for married taxpayers filing joint returns that is twice the range for single taxpayers. Thus, the phase-out range for married taxpayers filing jointly is between $190,000 and $220,000 of adjusted gross income. The 18–year old age ceiling on the eligible beneficiary was removed in the case of "special needs" children. In addition, § 530(b)(2) was amended to extend the exemption from tax to distributions for qualified elementary and secondary school expenses, including expenses of attending religious elementary and secondary schools, and the purchase of family computers. Finally, a taxpayer may both take advantage of the exclusion under § 530(d)(2) and claim the HOPE credit or Lifetime Learning Credit under § 25A, text, page 730, on behalf of the same student as long as the distributions from the account are not traced to the expenditures with respect to which the credit is claimed. I.R.C. § 25(d)(2)(C)(i). In other words, both benefits are available as long as qualified expenditures for the year equal or exceed the sum of the distributions from the account and the base on which the § 25A credit is calculated. Like all of the amendments in the 2001 Act, however, these changes sunset on December 31, 2010.

Page 344:

Omit the last two sentences of the carryover paragraph and insert:

Section 530(b)(1)(E) requires that any balance remaining in an EIRA on the beneficiary's 30th birthday, or death before attaining age 30, must be distributed within 30 days (unless a member of the beneficiary's family succeeds to his interest). Even if the distribution is not actually made, § 530(d)(8) deems it to have occurred. The distribution will be taxed as an annuity under § 72(b), subject to the 10 percent penalty tax on the amount includable in gross income under § 530(d)(4).

PART III

BUSINESS DEDUCTIONS AND CREDITS

CHAPTER 12

ORDINARY AND NECESSARY BUSINESS AND PROFIT-SEEKING EXPENSES

SECTION 2. THE "ORDINARY AND NECESSARY LIMITATION"

Page 362:

At the end of the carryover paragraph, insert:

However, § 62(a)(2)(D), enacted in 2002, which permits elementary and secondary school teachers to deduct up to $250 of § 162 expenses incurred for classroom books, supplies, and equipment (including computer equipment and software) in computing AGI (rather than as an itemized deduction) implicitly blesses such expenses as deductible business expenses notwithstanding the prior case law to the contrary.

Section 3. The Limitation of Unreasonable Compensation

Page 365:

At the end of the carryover paragraph, insert:

Most courts continue to apply multi-factor tests to determine the amount that constitutes reasonable compensation. See, e.g., LabelGraphics, Inc. v. Commissioner, 221 F.3d 1091 (9th Cir.2000), aff'g T.C. Memo. 1998–343. However, in Exacto Spring Corp. v. Commissioner, 196 F.3d 833 (7th Cir.1999), the Court of Appeals for the Seventh Circuit held that the only relevant inquiry is whether a hypothetical investor would be satisfied with the return on the investment that resulted from the employee/shareholder's management activities. According to *Exacto Spring*, if the hypothetical investor would have been satisfied with the return, then the compensation, whatever it might have been, is reasonable as long as it actually was intended to be compensation. In Eberl's Claim Service, Inc. v. Commissioner, 249 F.3d 994 (10th Cir.2001), the Court of Appeals for the Tenth Circuit expressly declined to follow the lead of the Eighth Circuit in *Exacto Spring Corp.* and held that the application of a multi-factor test remained the mode of analysis in reasonable compensation cases.

Pediatric Surgical Associates, P.C. v. Commissioner, T.C. Memo. 2001–81, raised an issue that affects many professional associations, including law firms doing business in the corporate form. The Tax Court upheld the disallowance of deductions for a portion of the bonuses to the four shareholder-employees of a medical professional corporation that had twenty employees, including two surgeons who were not shareholders. According to the court, the question was not only whether the amounts paid were reasonable, but whether they were actually received for services. Because the shareholder-physicians were not the only physicians, the amount that the physicians could have earned if self-employed was not completely determinative of the amount that would be reasonable compensation. Part of the shareholder-employee's bonuses represented the portion of the corporation's net profits (before the bonuses) attributable to the services of the nonshareholder-physicians. Accordingly, that portion of the bonuses was not paid to the shareholder-employee's as compensation for their services, but rather by virtue of their status as shareholders. That portion of the bonuses was not deductible.

SECTION 5. "PUBLIC POLICY" LIMITATIONS: TAX PENALTIES

A. BRIBES, FINES, AND PENALTIES

Page 380:

At the end of the citation to Talley Industries v. Commissioner, insert:

, on remand, T.C. Memo. 1999–200 (portion of $2.5 million settlement that exceed government's actual loss of $1.56 million represented double damages under the False Claims Act and was a nondeductible penalty), aff'd by order, 18 Fed.Appx. 661 (9th Cir.2001).

CHAPTER 13

DEDUCTIBLE PROFIT-SEEKING EXPENSES VERSUS NONDEDUCTIBLE CAPITAL EXPENDITURES

SECTION 1. EXPENDITURES TO ACQUIRE PROPERTY

Page 404:

After the third full paragraph, insert:

Rev. Rul. 2002–9, 2002–10 I.R.B. 614, held that under §§ 263(a) and 263A real estate developers must capitalize "impact fees" as costs allocable to the building. Impact fees are one-time charges imposed by a state or local government with respect to new or expanded real estate developments to finance offsite capital improvements for general public use, e.g., schools, parks, trunk roads, utilities, necessitated by the development.

Page 405:

After the second full paragraph, insert:

G. DE MINIMIS AMOUNTS

In Alacare Home Health Services Inc. v. Commissioner, T.C. Memo 2001–149, a Medicare-certified home health care agency deducted $800,000 of equipment purchases over two years. Each item of equipment cost $500 or less and had a life of two years or less. Expensing the equipment purchases was consistent with Medicare accounting rules. The Tax Court required the expenditures to be capitalized because the taxpayer's treatment did not clearly reflect income. The Tax Court distinguished Union Pacific Railroad Co. v. United States, 524 F.2d 1343, 208 Ct.Cl. 1 (1975), and Cincinnati, New Orleans & Tex. Pac. Railway Co. v. United States, 424 F.2d 563, 191 Ct.Cl. 572 (1970), both of which allowed a railroad to expense *de minimis* capital expenditures under an Interstate Commerce Commission directed accounting method, on the grounds that the deductions in those cases were a much lower percentage of gross receipts—.03% to .07% in the railroad cases compared with .85% and .71% in *Alacare*—and, unlike in *Alacare*, that the treatment in the railroad cases clearly reflected income.

SECTION 2. EXPENDITURES WITH BENEFIT BEYOND THE TAXABLE YEAR

Page 411:

After the carryover paragraph, insert:

FMR Corp. v. Commissioner, 110 T.C. 402 (1998), was a significant application of *INDOPCO* where the *Lincoln Savings* separate and distinct asset test could not easily be applied. The case involved the treatment of expenditures incurred by the taxpayer, which was the fund manager of the Fidelity Fund family of mutual funds, to form 82 additional mutual funds, increasing the total number of funds to approximately 140 funds. The new mutual funds were established as separate legal entities, which had perpetual existence, and the taxpayer was the sole underwriter and distributor of shares in them. The taxpayer did not own the funds or their assets—the investors did—but the taxpayer expected to, and did, earn significant profits over an extended number of years from marketing and managing the funds. The court specifically applied only the *INDOPCO* "future benefits" analysis to require capitalization of the expenditures.

After the first full paragraph, insert:

In most cases the separate and distinct asset test of *Lincoln Savings* and the future benefit test of *INDOPCO* are closely related. PNC Bancorp, Inc. v. Commissioner, 110 T.C. 349 (1998), involved whether loan origination costs routinely incurred by a bank in making both consumer and commercial loans were ordinary and necessary business expenses or capital expenditures. The expenditures in question included not only payments to third parties for credit reports, appraisals, and costs of recording security interests, but also an allocable portion of the salary and benefits of employees attributable to evaluating loan applications, negotiating, processing and closing loans, and recording security arrangements with respect to loans that were made by the banks. The Tax Court's opinion requiring capitalization of the expenses in question reflects both approaches:

"Credit reports, appraisals, and similar information about prospective borrowers are critical in deciding whether to make a loan. * * * While the specific information available when a loan is made may become outdated in a relatively short period of time, the quality of the decision to make a loan (and thereby acquire an asset) is predicated on such information. The soundness of the decision to make a loan is assimilated into the quality and value of the loan. Thus, the direct costs of the decision-making process should be assimilated into the asset that was acquired. * * *

"Costs associated with the origination of the loans contribute to the generation of interest income and provide a long-term benefit that the banks realize over the lives of the underlying loans. The resulting stream of income extends well beyond the year in which the costs were incurred. It was this income benefit that was the primary purpose for incurring these expenditures. While the useful life of a credit report and other financial data may be of short duration, the useful life of the asset they serve to create is not. * * *

"The costs at issue are directly connected to the creation of loans, which constitute separate and distinct assets that are the banks' primary source of income. Revenues, in the form of interest payments, are received over the life of the individual loans. In order to accurately measure the banks's net income, the direct costs of originating the loans must be capitalized and amortized over the life of the loans."

On appeal, however, the Tax Court's decision was reversed, and a current deduction was allowed. 212 F.3d 822 (3d Cir.2000). The Court of Appeals reasoned that because interest on loans was the bank's largest revenue source, the loans in question were not "separate and distinct assets." According to the court, the loan origination costs thus were merely the normal and routine costs of doing business, which were not subject to capitalization. The court distinguished *Lincoln Savings* on the grounds that the "Secondary Reserve fund," to which Lincoln Savings made the payments and which was the separate asset in that case, existed wholly apart from Lincoln Savings' business and that because PNC's payments did not become part of the balance of the loan, PNC's origination activities did not "create" the loans in the way Lincoln Savings' payments created the Secondary Reserve fund. The court found that *INDOPCO* principles did not require capitalization because the future benefit test was not intended by the Supreme Court to be talismanic in all cases, and, it reasoned, although the loans themselves may have had lives of several years, the information obtained by the bank as a result of the original fees had a relatively short life.

While it is true that consumer and commercial loan origination is the ordinary everyday activity of a bank and the regularity of the expenses might limit somewhat the potential for distortion, it is equally true that manufacturing cars, the cost of which clearly must be capitalized through an inventory accounting method, is the ordinary everyday activity of Ford. Likewise, while the court of appeals may be correct that the credit check and other information gathered in the loan origination process has a life that lasts only until it is used, and thus the expenses to obtain that benefit might be said to have limited future benefit, the same is also true with respect to expenses incurred in a title search of real estate to be purchased, and those expenses clearly must be capitalized. Finally, *Commissioner v. Idaho Power Co.*, text, page 403, indicates that the proper focus of the inquiry is not confined merely to the period over which the information obtained as a result of the loan origination expenditures would be used directly. That information, which itself might have had a short life, was a cost of producing the loans, just as the depreciation on the relatively short-lived construction equipment in *Idaho Power* was a cost of the long-lived power plant.

Notwithstanding the reversal by the Third Circuit in *PNC Bancorp*, the Tax Court still believes in the capitalization requirement. Lychuk v. Commissioner, 116 T.C. 374 (2001), involved a taxpayer in the of business of acquiring and servicing multi-year installment contracts from used car dealers. It acquired each contract at a discount from face value and thereafter collected and kept all payments. Its business activities consisted of credit investigation and evaluation, documenting transactions, and collecting on the installment contracts. The taxpayer acquired and serviced less than one half of the contracts offered to it by automobile dealers. Several employees were engaged in determining which contracts to acquire, and the taxpayer deducted all of its expenses for this activity, including the employees' salaries. The Commissioner determined that all of the salaries, benefits, and overhead (printing, telephone, computer, rent, and utilities) relating to the corporation's acquisition of the installment contracts were capital expenditures, but did not require capitalization of the salaries, benefits, and overhead attributable to servicing the contracts. The Tax Court held that the employees' salaries and benefits were capital expenditures because the items were directly related to the process of anticipated acquisition of assets with expected useful lives exceeding one year. The court's opinion was grounded on the principles of *Lincoln Savings and Loan Ass'n*, text, page 410, *Idaho Power Co.*, text, page 403, and *Woodward*, text, page 399. The Tax Court expressly rejected the Third Circuit's holding *PNC Bancorp, Inc.* and followed its own prior opinion in that case. Nevertheless, the Tax Court allowed a current deduction for the overhead expenses because these items were not directly related to the anticipated acquisitions—they would have been incurred even if the corporation's business had only encompassed servicing the contracts, and their amount did not vary with the number of credit applications processed—and any future benefit received from these expenses was merely "incidental." A loss deduction under § 165(a) was allowed with respect to the portion of the capitalized salaries and benefits that was attributable to installment contracts that were never acquired. Seven judges concurred with the court's opinion requiring that the salaries and benefits be capitalized, but dissented from the portion of the opinion allowing the overhead to be deducted. The dissenters would have required capitalization of the overhead as well.

The Treasury Department has announced its intention to surrender on the issue of loan origination costs by following the Third Circuit's opinion in *PNC Bancorp,* allowing current deductions, notwithstanding that the Tax Court held in *Lychuk* that it would continue to require capitalization of loan origination costs. In an Advanced Notice of Proposed Rulemaking ("ANPRM"), REG–125638–01, Guidance Regarding Deduction and Capitalization of Expenditures, 67 F.R. 3461 (1/24/02), the Treasury Department announced that it would promulgate regulations under which such costs would be currently deductible; the amount of the loan advanced, of course, would remain subject to capitalization.

Page 412:

After the fourth sentence of the first full paragraph, insert:

Rev. Rul. 98–25, 1998–1 C.B. 998, is in a similar vein. In the Ruling, the taxpayer removed, emptied, cleaned, and disposed of old steel underground storage tanks containing manufacturing waste by-products. It also acquired, installed, and filled new steel-fiberglass-reenforced plastic underground storage tanks to contain the manufacturing waste by-products for an indefinite period of time. The Service ruled that the new storage tanks, which had no salvage value, had no useful life to the taxpayer beyond the year and thus were analogous to materials and supplies. An immediate deduction was allowed for all of the costs. Rev. Rul. 98–25 distinguished Rev. Rul. 94–38, text, page 412, on the basis that the groundwater treatment facility in the earlier Ruling was used by the taxpayer beyond the year in question. The distinction is difficult to see. But see Dominion Resources, Inc. v. United States, 219 F.3d 359 (4th Cir.2000) (environmental remediation costs were required to be capitalized because they were incurred for the purpose of preparing property retired from use as electric power plant for sale or use as an office site and increased its appraised value from approximately $1.5 million to approximately $9 million).

Page 412:

After the first full paragraph, insert:

A1. PROPOSED *INDOPCO* REGULATIONS

In late 2002, the Treasury Department published Prop. Reg. § 1.263(a)–4 (2002), which, when finalized, will deal comprehensively with the capitalization of expenditures that relate to intangible assets and "future benefits." Although commonly referred to as the *INDOPCO* regulations, because they are intended to provide bright-line rules to make the standards based approach to capitalization articulated by the Supreme Court in *INDOPCO*, text, page 405, more administrable, the regulations might more properly be called the anti-*INDOPCO* regulations, because they reverse the principle, if not the specific holding, of *INDOPCO*.

The Supreme Court in *INDOPCO* unequivocally rejected the view that capitalization was not required unless the expenditure resulted in the creation or improvement of a "separate and distinct asset," and also clearly announced that "the notion that deductions are exceptions to the norm of capitalization" is embodied in various aspects of the Code and is supported by a long line of Supreme Court precedents. The proposed regulations turn on their head these interpretations of §§ 162, 261, and 263 by the Supreme Court.

Under Prop. Reg. § 1.263(a)–4(b)(1) (2002), the only expenditures that must be capitalized are those incurred (1) to acquire, create, or enhance an intangible asset, (2) to facilitate in the acquisition, creation, or enhancement of an intangible asset, (3) to facilitate a restructuring or reorganization of a business entity or a transaction involving the acquisition of capital, including a stock issuance, borrowing, or recapitalization,[1] or (4) that are otherwise identified by the IRS in prospectively effective published guidance. The term "separate and distinct intangible asset" is limited by Prop. Reg. § 1.263(a)–4(b)(3) (2002) to "a property interest of ascertainable and measurable value in money's worth that is subject to protection under applicable state or federal law and the possession and control of which is intrinsically capable of being sold, transferred, or pledged (ignoring any restrictions imposed on assignability)."[2] The only expenses not related to a separate and distinct asset that must be capitalized under the proposed regulations are costs to "facilitate . . . a restructuring or reorganization of a business entity or a transaction involving the acquisition of capital, including a stock issuance, borrowing, or recapitalization." This category includes only fact patterns analogous to the narrow fact pattern in *INDOPCO* and a number of cases involving similar issues that followed *INDOPCO*. Thus, the future benefits test of *INDOPCO* has been largely abandoned. See, e.g., Prop. Reg. § 1.263(a)–4(d)(4) (2002) (expenses for certification of products, services or business processes are not subject to capitalization).

The proposed regulations provide two very important exceptions to the rule requiring capitalization of transaction costs. First, under a "simplifying convention" that is in fact a major substantive rule, Prop. Reg. § 1.263(a)–4(e)(3) (2002) provides that compensation paid to employees and the employer's associated overhead are never capitalized. This provision rejects case law to the contrary and goes far beyond the principle of those cases that in certain circumstances have allowed a current deduction for employee compensation that facilitates the acquisition of an intangible asset.[3] Moreover, it adopts a rule for dealing with intangible assets that is diametrically opposed to the treatment of transaction costs with respect to

1. Prop. Reg. § 1.263(a)–4(e)(4) (2002) provides special rules relating to transaction costs relating to the acquisition of a business or a corporate reorganization. Transaction costs incurred by a corporation to defend against a hostile takeover are not required to be capitalized, because they do not facilitate an acquisition. But expenses incurred to thwart a hostile acquisition by merging with a white knight or recapitalizing must be capitalized. Prop. Reg. § 1.263(a)–4(e)(4)(iii) (2002).

2. See also Prop. Reg. § 1.263(a)–4(b)(2) (defining "intangible assets"); Prop. Reg. § 1.263(a)–4(c) (2002) (listing intangible assets the cost of which must be capitalized if acquired from another person); Prop. Reg. § 1.263(a)–4(c) (2002) (listing self-created intangible assets, including prepaid expenses, the cost of which must be capitalized).

3. See Norwest Corp. v. Commissioner, 112 T.C. 89 (1999) (disallowing deduction), rev'd sub nom., Wells Fargo & Co. v. Commissioner, 224 F.3d 874 (8th Cir.2000); PNC Bancorp, Inc. v. Commissioner, 110 T.C. 349 (1998) (disallowing deduction), rev'd, 212 F.3d 822 (3d Cir.2000); Lychuk v. Commissioner, 116 T.C. 374 (2001) (disallowing deduction), all discussed supra, page 49.

tangible assets, which always must be capitalized under either or both of §§ 263(a) or 263A, see text, pages 402–405.

Second, Prop. Reg. § 1.263(a)–4(e)(3)(2002) provides an exception that permits *de minimis* transaction costs—defined as costs that do not exceed $5,000 per transaction (not per payee)—to be deducted currently. Because this rule is coupled with an elective average cost pooling method, the *de minimis* rule is subject to substantial manipulation and can result in current deductions for very significant transaction costs.[4]

In the preamble to the proposed regulations, the Treasury Department explains that "the separate and distinct asset standard has not historically yielded the same level of controversy as the significant future benefit standard," and that "the separate and distinct asset test is a workable principle in practice." REG–125638–01, Guidance Regarding Deduction and Capitalization of Expenditures, 67 FR 77701 (Dec. 19, 2002) The preamble also explains that the IRS and Treasury Department might in the future identify expenditures that are not listed in the regulations, but for which capitalization is nonetheless appropriate. Capitalization of non-listed expenditures will be required, however, only if (and after) they have been identified in published guidance. Unless an expenditure relating to an intangible asset is listed in the regulations or in such subsequently published guidance, however, capitalization will not be required and a current deduction will be allowed. Thus, under the proposed regulations, capitalization will become an exception to the norm of deducting business expenditures.

Finally, Prop. Reg. § 1.167(a)–3(b) (2002) provides a fifteen-year "safe-harbor" amortization period for any capitalized expenses relating to a self-created intangible for which another amortization period is not prescribed by the Code or regulations and for which amortization is not proscribed.

Page 415:

After the first full paragraph, insert:

Treas. Reg. § 1.195–1 requires that an election to amortize start-up costs under § 195 specify the expenses with respect to which the election applies and prohibits an amended election from including any expenses with respect to which the taxpayer has taken a return position treating the expenses as currently deductible rather than as a capitalized and amortizable start-up expense. This rule is designed to prevent taxpayers from playing the audit lottery on start-up costs by aggressively claiming them as deductible expenses, confident that if they lose, the worst result is 60 month amortization. Under the Regulations, if the taxpayer erroneously claims a start-up expense as a deduction, the start-up never can be amortized under § 195 even though the deduction is disallowed.

4. Prop. Reg. § 1.263(a)–4(e)(3)(C) (2002).

Prop. Reg. § 1.263(a)–4(e)(4) (2002) provides a "bright-line rule" for differentiating transaction cost expenditures subject to § 195 and expenditures that are inherently capital as costs of the acquisition of the business itself. Expenses incurred in the process of pursuing an acquisition of a trade or business (whether the acquisition is structured as an acquisition of stock or of assets and whether the taxpayer is the acquirer in the acquisition or the target of the acquisition) must be capitalized only if (1) they are "inherently facilitative" of the acquisition or (2) if they relate to activities performed after the earlier of the date a letter of intent (or similar communication) is issued (or, if the taxpayer is a corporation, the date the board of directors approves the acquisition proposal). Expenditures that are "inherently facilitative" include amounts expended to determine the value of the target, drafting transactional documents, or conveying property between the parties. Under this bright-line rule, expenditures that do not facilitate the acquisition are subject to § 195. Of course, the actual cost of the business itself, whether structured as a stock or asset acquisition, is a capital expense.

Page 417:

After the third full paragraph, insert:

The Tax Court's decision in FMR Corp. v. Commissioner, page 43, implicitly questions the continuing post-*INDOPCO* precedential value of the cases allowing deductions for "business expansion" costs. The taxpayer argued that by expanding the family of mutual funds it managed, it was preserving and expanding its existing business and that such expenses were clearly deductible under *NCNB Corporation*, text at page 417, and similar cases. In rejecting the taxpayer's argument, the court distinguished those cases as pre-*INDOPCO* law, which drew distinctions that *INDOPCO* was intended to resolve. The court also rejected the taxpayer's argument that in enacting § 195 Congress explicitly recognized that business "expansion" costs always were currently deductible. According to the Tax Court, § 195 allows amortization only of those start-up costs that would have been deductible under other principles if they were incurred by a going business, and business expansion costs are either deductible or capitalized case-by-case under a facts and circumstances test. Subsequently, in Norwest Corp. v. Commissioner, 112 T.C. 89 (1999), the Tax Court directly held that *INDOPCO* had effectively overruled the line of cases, including *NCNB Corp.*, that allowed a current deduction for "business expansion" costs, in contrast to start-up costs. The court concluded that the enactment of § 195 did not implicitly endorse the deductibility of all business expansion costs. On appeal, however, the Court of Appeals for the Eighth Circuit reversed the Tax Court's decision in *Norwest sub nom*, Wells Fargo & Co. v. Commissioner, 224 F.3d 874 (8th Cir.2000). In issuing Rev. Rul. 99–23, page 37, the Service appears to have conceded that expenses to investigate business expansion in the same line of business can be currently deductible.

Deductible business expansion expenses do not include, however, the actual cost of business assets or the cost of acquiring the stock of a corporation. Thus, for example, in American Stores Co. v. Commissioner, 114 T.C. 458 (2000), the taxpayer was required to capitalize legal fees incurred in defending an antitrust suit challenging the taxpayer's proposed acquisition of another corporation because they were paid in connection with an acquisition.

Page 418:

At the end of the first full paragraph, insert:

In USFreightways Corp. v. Commissioner, 113 T.C. 329 (1999), the Tax Court held that if an expenditure incurred by an accrual method taxpayer provides a benefit for a period that does not exceed twelve months but which straddles two taxable years, the portion of the expenditure relating to the year subsequent to the year in which it was incurred must be capitalized pursuant to § 263. The Seventh Circuit reversed the Tax Court's decision that § 263 required the deduction to be prorated over the two taxable years. 270 F.3d 1137 (7th Cir.2001). The Court of Appeals concluded that the Tax Court's decision that the capitalization rules could apply differently to cash method and accrual method taxpayers, which resulted in capitalizing USFreightways' expenses when like expenses of a cash method taxpayer might not have been required to be capitalized, was untenable. The Court of Appeals remanded the case to the Tax Court to consider whether the deduction nevertheless should be prorated over the two taxable years under the "clear reflection of income" standard of § 446(b).

The Treasury Department has announced its intention to surrender on the issue in *USFreightways*. Prop. Reg. § 1.263(a)–4(f) (2002) would provide that an expenditure to create or enhance intangible rights or benefits that do not extend for more than twelve months after the expenditure is incurred is not required to be capitalized. Prepaid expenses covering a period of more than twelve months would continue to be capitalized in full and deducted ratably over the period benefitted. When determining the duration of a right, renewal periods must be taken into account if the facts and circumstances indicate a reasonable expectancy of renewal. Prop. Reg. § 1.263(a)–4(f)(5) (2002). This arbitrary line produces unusual results. Suppose that in March 2002, Taxpayer *A* pays an insurance premium of $130,000 for the period from April 1, 2002 through April 30, 2003. Taxpayer *B*, on the other hand, in December 2002, pays an insurance premium of $120,000 for the period from December 1, 2002 through November 30, 2003. For 2002, Taxpayer *A*'s deduction is $90,000. Taxpayer *B*'s deduction for 2002, however, is $120,000, even though Taxpayer *B*'s prepayment extends further into 2003 than does Taxpayer *A*'s prepayment.

In Steger v. Commissioner, 113 T.C. 227 (1999), the cost of a multi-year nonpracticing malpractice insurance policy to cover post-retirement claims arising out of preretirement work purchased by a retiring cash method lawyer in the last year of conducting a law practice was currently deductible as a cost of closing his business. The result in *Steger* can be justified because even though the insurance policy covered multiple years, it was a deferred expense that related to income earned in prior years that had already been taxed.

SECTION 3. IMPROVEMENT VERSUS REPAIR OR REPLACEMENT

Page 427:

At the end of the carryover paragraph, insert:

The governing standard probably is best encapsulated as requiring capitalization if the repair is the replacement of a crucial portion of the asset that has a distinct useful life shorter than the remaining life of the larger integrated asset of which it is a portion and the cost of the replacement is a substantial (but not necessarily even approaching a majority) percentage of the overall cost of the entire asset. See Smith v. Commissioner, 300 F.3d 1023 (9th Cir.2002) (the cost of replacing portions of equipment used in aluminum smelting was a capital expense); Ingram Industries Inc. v. Commissioner, T.C. Memo. 2000–323 (expenses for periodic maintenance of inland barge towboat engines were deductible as repairs rather than being capital expenses because the engines were not separate property from the boats themselves, the work was not the equivalent of completely rebuilding or overhauling the engines, and there was no way to measure any increment in value of a boat resulting from the maintenance).

After the third full paragraph, insert:

Dominion Resources, Inc. v. United States, 219 F.3d 359 (4th Cir. 2000), is another case in which expenses were required to be capitalized rather than being deductible as repairs. To prepare the site of a retired power plant for use as an office building site or for sale, the taxpayer incurred environmental remediation expenses to remove asbestos and other contaminants from the site. Rev. Rul. 94–38, 1994–1 C.B. 35, text, page 412, generally allows a deduction for environmental remediation costs to remedy the taxpayer's own prior pollution. In *Dominion Resources*, however, the taxpayer was required to capitalize the expenditures because the remediation altered the character of the property by enabling it to be put to "a wide range of new uses" as opposed to merely keeping the property in its ordinary efficient condition or restoring it to a condition that existed prior to deterioration or damage.

Dominion Resources was followed in United Dairy Farmers, Inc. v. United States, 267 F.3d 510 (6th Cir.2001). The taxpayer incurred environmental remediation expenses to clean up pollution caused by prior owners who operated gas stations on the site of a convenience store. Even though the taxpayer was unaware of the pollution at the time of the purchase and thus "overpaid" for the property, it was required to capitalize the expenses because they "increased the value of the property." Rev. Rul. 94–38 did not apply. The Sixth Circuit concluded that "when a taxpayer improves property defects that were present when the taxpayer acquired the property, the remediation of those defects are capital in nature."

Cinergy Corp. v. United States, 55 Fed.Cl. 489 (2003), allowed a § 162 repair deduction for the cost of removing and encapsulating deteriorating fireproofing material that contained asbestos fibers. The fireproofing material did not create a problem for years, but as it deteriorated the danger of the asbestos circulating in the offices increased. The work prevented the asbestos from crumbling or circulating. In allowing the deduction, the court applied the test used by the Sixth Circuit in *United Dairy Farmers, Inc. v. United States*, supra, and found all of the elements to be met.

> [T]hree elements must be satisfied for a valid deduction under § 162 for environmental cleanup costs: first, the taxpayer contaminated the property in its ordinary course of business; second, the taxpayer cleaned up the contamination to restore the property to its pre-contamination state; third, the cleanup did not allow the taxpayer to put the property to a new use.

The court distinguished *United Dairy Farmers, Inc.,* in which the taxpayer acquired the property after it had been contaminated, and *Dominion Resources, Inc. v. Unites States*, supra, in which the environmental remediation adapted the property for a different use.

For years to which the current version of § 198, text, page 366 and this supplement, page 64, applies, the environmental remediation expenses in *Dominion Resources* and *United Dairy Farmers* would be deductible if the site had been certified by the appropriate state environmental agency as the location where there had been a release of a "hazardous substance."

Page 428:

After the last paragraph, insert:

In Rev. Rul. 2001–4, 2001–1 C.B. 295, the Service provided significant guidance regarding the dividing line between repair costs deductible under § 162 and replacement and rehabilitation costs that must be capitalized. The ruling dealt with costs incurred by an airline with respect to "heavy maintenance" of aircraft performed every eight years in three specific situations involving fully depreciated aircraft. At the time the aircraft were placed in service, it was anticipated that, if maintained, they would be useful for up to 25 years, although they are depreciable under §§ 167 and 168 over seven years. The ruling holds that heavy maintenance expenses generally are deductible, but costs incurred in conjunction with a heavy maintenance must be capitalized to the extent that the costs materially add to the value of the aircraft, substantially prolong its useful life, or adapt it to a new or different use. Any costs incurred as part of a plan of rehabilitation, modernization, or improvement also must be capitalized. In the first situation, a heavy maintenance, which took 45 days, was performed for the purpose of preventing deterioration of the inherent safety and reliability levels of the aircraft. The aircraft was substantially disassembled, inspected, repaired, and reassembled, after which it was tested, and returned to service. Although numerous parts were replaced, the maintenance work did not extend the useful life of the aircraft beyond the originally anticipated 25–year useful life, but merely kept it in an efficient operating condition. It was used for the same purposes and in the same manner as prior to the maintenance. The expenses for this heavy maintenance were fully deductible. In the second example, wear and corrosion of the aircraft fuselage required replacement of a significant portion of all of the exterior fuselage panels, and the work performed materially added to the aircraft's value. In addition, while the aircraft was disassembled, it was upgraded by the installation of a cabin smoke and fire detection and suppression system, a ground proximity warning system, and an air phone system to enable passengers to send and receive voice calls, faxes, and other electronic data while in flight. The expenses incurred with respect to this aircraft had to be allocated between the deductible heavy maintenance, on the one hand and the skin replacement and electrical upgrades, which had to be capitalized, on the other hand. In the third situation, the aircraft, which was 22 years old and nearing the end of its anticipated useful life, was substantially improved to increase its reliability and extend its useful life. With respect to this aircraft, all of the expenses, including those that otherwise would have been deductible routine heavy maintenance expenses, had to be capitalized as part of a plan of general rehabilitation and modernization that materially increased the aircraft's value and life.

CHAPTER 14

COST RECOVERY MECHANISMS

SECTION 1. DEPRECIATION

Page 450:

After the carryover paragraph, insert:

In O'Shaughnessy v. Commissioner, 89 A.F.T.R.2d 2002–658 (D.Minn. 2001), the taxpayer manufactured glass using a "float process" that involved the use of a molten tin "bath" that lost volume and purity in the manufacturing process, requiring periodic replenishment. The amount of tin added each year equaled the amount of tin consumed in glass production during the year. The taxpayer both deducted the cost of adding tin to the bath and depreciated the cost of the original volume of tin. Applying Rev. Rul. 75–491, 1975–2 C.B. 19, which was directly on point, the Service disallowed the depreciation. The district court refused to apply the revenue ruling, because it was not binding and because it predated the ACRS depreciation system, and held that the original volume of tin was depreciable because over time it would have been completely exhausted by volume and purity losses. By allowing the taxpayer both to deduct, rather than capitalize, the cost of replenishing the tin lost in the production process and to depreciate the original volume of tin, this decision, in effect, permitted the taxpayer to deduct the cost of a non-wasting asset.

At the end of the first full paragraph, insert:

Rev. Rul. 2001–60, 2001–51 I.R.B. 587, dealt with depreciation of golf course land improvements. Land preparation undertaken in the original construction or reconstruction of "push-up" or natural soil greens is inextricably associated with the land and, therefore, the costs attributable to that land preparation are not depreciable. However, the costs of land preparation of "modern" greens, which are constructed with a network of underground drainage tiles or pipes, are closely associated with those depreciable assets. Since the land preparation will be retired, abandoned, or replaced contemporaneously with those tiles and pipes, the land preparation costs are to be capitalized and depreciated over the recovery period of the associated depreciable assets.

After the third full paragraph, insert:

3. *Intangible Assets*

Prop. Reg. § 1.167(a)–3(b) (2002) would permit amortization of the basis of most intangibles that do not have readily ascertainable useful lives and for which a specific amortization or depreciation period is not specified in the Code or regulations, and for which amortization or depreciation is not proscribed. Unless the Service provides a different amortization period by published guidance, the "safe-harbor" amortization period is fifteen years, using a straight-line method with no salvage value. Thus, for example, an amount paid to obtain a trade association membership of indefinite duration would be amortizable over fifteen years. The amortization rule does not apply to intangible assets acquired from another party or to self-created financial interests, but these intangibles may be amortizable under § 197 or under other provisions of the Code or regulations. See text, page 458. Intangibles that have a readily ascertainable useful life are amortized over that life. See text page 462–63.

Page 456:

After the third full paragraph, insert:

4A. *Additional First Year Recovery*

Section 168(k)(1) and (k)(4), added by the 2002 Act and 2003 Act, respectively, as an additional stimulus to capital investment, allow a deduction of thirty percent of the adjusted basis of qualified property placed in service after September 10, 2001 and before May 6, 2003, and a deduction of fifty percent of the adjusted basis of qualified property placed in service after May 5, 2003 and before January 1, 2005. The adjusted basis of qualified property for purposes of calculating otherwise allowable depreciation is reduced by the first year deduction. I.R.C. § 168(k)(1)(B). This basis adjustment is taken into account before computing the otherwise normal annual depreciation allowances.

Qualified property is defined in § 168(k)(2) as any property with a recovery period of 20 years or less (3, 5, 7, 10, 15, and 20 year MACRS property), computer software that is eligible for 36 month capital recovery under § 167(f)(1)(B), water utility property that is defined in § 168(e)(5), and qualified leasehold improvement property. Qualified leasehold improvement property includes tenant or lessor improvements to the interior of nonresidential real property that are placed in service more than three years after the building is placed in service. I.R.C. § 168(k)(3)(A). Qualified leasehold improvement property does not include an enlargement of the building, elevators or escalators, a structural improvement to a common area, or the internal structural framework of the building. I.R.C. § 168(k)(3)(B). To qualify for the first year deduction, leasehold improvements must be made pursuant to a lease, which is defined as any grant of a right to use property. I.R.C. § 168(k)(3)(A)(i), (h)(7).

The first year deduction is allowed only for qualified property the original use of which commences with the taxpayer. I.R.C. § 168(k)(2)(A)(ii). The Staff of the Joint Committee on Taxation, Explanation of the "Job Creation and Worker Assistance Act of 2002", at 3, n.5 (JCX–12–02, 2002), explains the original use requirement as follows:

> The term "original use" means the first use to which the property is put, whether or not such use corresponds to the use of such property by the taxpayer. It is intended that, when evaluating whether property qualifies as "original use," the factors used to determine whether property qualified as "new section 38 property" for purposes of the investment tax credit would apply. See Treasury Regulation 1.48–2. Thus, it is intended that additional capital expenditures incurred to recondition or rebuild acquired property (or owned property) would satisfy the "original use" requirement. However, the cost of reconditioned or rebuilt property acquired by the taxpayer would not satisfy the "original use" requirement. For example, if on February 1, 2002, a taxpayer buys from X for $20,000 a machine that has been previously used by X. Prior to September 11, 2004, the taxpayer makes an expenditure on the property of $5,000 of the type that must be capitalized. Regardless of whether the $5,000 is added to the basis of such property or is capitalized as a separate asset, such amount would be treated as satisfying the "original use" requirement and would be qualified property (assuming all other conditions are met). No part of the $20,000 purchase price would qualify for the additional first year depreciation.

The regulations referred to in the Joint Committee report contain factors for determining original use under the 10 percent investment tax credit of § 38, which was eliminated in 1986.

Qualified property also includes self-constructed tangible property with an estimated production period in excess of two years, or in excess of one year with a cost in excess of $1,000,000, as described in § 263A(f)(1)(B)(ii) & (iii), that has a recovery period of at least 10 years or that is used in the trade or business of transporting persons or property ("transportation property"). I.R.C. § 168(k)(2)(B)(i)(I) & (ii). Property that is required to be depreciated under the alternative depreciation system of § 168(g), text, page 456 is not eligible for the 30 percent first year write-off of § 168(k).

Section 168(k)(2)(F) provides that the 50 percent (and 30 percent) first year allowance is also allowable as a deduction for purposes of the alternative minimum tax, discussed in Chapter 36.

SECTION 2. STATUTORY AMORTIZATION OF INTANGIBLE ASSETS

Page 458:

In the Regulations citations, insert:

Sections 1.167(a)–14(b), (c); 1.197–2.

Page 462:

Replace the first full paragraph with the following:

Section 197(c)(2) generally limits the application of the fifteen-year amortization rule to the following self-created assets: (1) licenses, permits, and other rights granted by a governmental authority, for example, a liquor license or taxi medallion, (2) franchises (as defined in § 1253(b)(1)), trade-names, or trademarks, and (3) covenants not to complete. Thus for example, because a patent is not listed in § 197(c)(2), any capitalized costs relating to a self-created patent—in contrast to a patent purchased as part of a going business—would be depreciable over the life of the patent as under prior law. Likewise, self-created copyrights on computer software are depreciable over 36 months under § 167(f)(1). On the other hand, a covenant not to compete must be amortized over 15 years under § 197, regardless of the term of the covenant or the period over which payments are made, even if the covenant is entered into pursuant to the acquisition of the interest of one of the owners of a business by the remaining owner. See Frontier Chevrolet Co. v. Commissioner, 116 T.C. 289 (2001) (§ 197 applied to a covenant not to compete entered into when a corporation redeemed the stock of a 75–percent owner).

Page 463:

In the sixth line of the first full paragraph, **replace the citation to** "Prop. Reg. § 1.167(a)–14(c)(4)" **with** "Treas. Reg. § 1.167(a)–14(c)(4)."

In the twelfth and thirteenth lines of the second full paragraph, replace the citation to "Prop. Reg. § 1.197–2(g)(1)(i)(A)" **with** "Treas. Reg. § 1.197–2(g)(1)(i)(A)."

SECTION 3. EXPENSING AND AMORTIZATION PROVISIONS

Page 464:

After the third sentence of the paragraph headed, "A. ELECTION TO EXPENSES CERTAIN DEPRECIABLE BUSINESS ASSETS," insert:

The 2003 Act increased the amount deductible under § 179 to $100,000 for property placed in service in taxable years beginning in 2003, 2004, and 2005. In addition, for those years, the dollar-for-dollar phase-out of the amount begins when the cost of property placed in service exceeds $400,000 (adjusted for inflation in 2004 and 2005). The 2003 Act also amended § 179(d) to treat off-the-shelf computer software placed in service in taxable years beginning in 2003 through 2005 as qualifying property.

After the third full paragraph, insert:

Under Treas. Reg. § 1.179–5(a), an election to expense otherwise depreciable assets under § 179 must be made on the taxpayer's first return for the year or on a timely amended return, and cannot be modified without the Commissioner's consent. In Patton v. Commissioner, 116 T.C. 206 (2001), the taxpayer elected to expense a single $4,100 asset. On audit, items that the taxpayer had deducted as "supplies" were reclassified as capital expenditures. The taxpayer attempted to modify the original election to extend it to the capital expenditures determined after the audit, but the court held that the Commissioner did not unreasonably withhold consent to modification of the original election. This is an example of an instance where aggressive reporting on the return forecloses a subsequent claim of an otherwise available tax benefit that validly could have been claimed at the outset. The 2003 Act amended § 179(c)(2) to allow elections to expense assets under § 179 with respect to taxable years beginning in 2003 through 2005 to be revoked (by an amended return) without the consent of the Commissioner.

Page 466:

At the end of the second full paragraph, insert:

As amended in 2000 and 2001, § 198 allows a deduction for any environmental remediation expenses that relate to a site (1) held by the taxpayer for use in the taxpayer's trade or business or for sale to customers, and (2) that has been designated by an appropriate state or federal environmental agency as a site where there has been a release (or a threat of release) or disposal of a hazardous substance. The statute sets forth standards for identifying "hazardous substances." However, sites designated under the Comprehensive Environmental Response, Compensation, and Liability Act of 1980 (CERCLA) do not qualify. IRC § 198(c)(2). Section 198 is scheduled to sunset after December 31, 2003, but in all likelihood, its life will be extended again. In a nation supposedly concerned with its environment, and which believes that every problem can be solved by a tax deduction or credit, § 198 is most likely destined to have an eternal life.

SECTION 4. CAPITAL RECOVERY FOR NATURAL RESOURCES

Page 468:

At the end of the last paragraph, insert:

Special rules also apply to percentage depletion for "marginal production," as defined in § 613A(c)(6). See I.R.C. § 613A(c)(6)(H).

CHAPTER 15

TRANSACTIONAL LOSSES

SECTION 1. DETERMINING THE AMOUNT OF BUSINESS OR PROFIT SEEKING LOSS

Page 480:

At the end of the first full paragraph, insert:

In Trinity Meadows Raceway, Inc. v. Commissioner, 187 F.3d 638 (6th Cir.1999), the taxpayer's racetrack and parking lot were damaged by a flood. No loss deduction was allowed because the taxpayer's calculations were based on the aggregate basis of the racetrack and parking lot and the aggregate diminution in fair market value, and the evidence did not reveal either the basis or the diminution in the fair market value of each separately identifiable asset damaged by the flood.

SECTION 2. REQUIREMENT OF "CLOSED AND COMPLETED TRANSACTION" AND "NOT COMPENSATED BY INSURANCE OR OTHERWISE" LIMITATION

Page 488:

After the last paragraph, insert:

In contrast, in Gates v. United States, 81 A.F.T.R.2d 98-1622 (M.D.Pa. 1998), aff'd by order, 168 F.3d 478 (3d Cir.1998), § 280B was applied to deny the taxpayer a loss with respect to the demolition of a building three years after it was vandalized and found to contain asbestos. The taxpayer had purchased and held the building as a speculative investment, never having leased it out. The court held that to avoid the disallowance rule of § 280B, the taxpayer must demonstrate either sudden obsolescence or an affirmative act of abandonment. If the building had become suddenly worthless by virtue of vandalism and the discovery of asbestos, the proper year for a deduction would have been the year in which those events occurred, not the subsequent year in which it was demolished. The taxpayer never demonstrated an act of abandonment prior to the building's demolition. See also Norwest Corp. v. Commissioner, 111 T.C. 105 (1998) (disallowing a claimed worthlessness deduction with respect to a building because there was no act of abandonment evidencing a closed and completed transaction).

SECTION 4. BAD DEBTS

Page 500:

At the end of the first full paragraph, insert:

Although, as was observed by the court in Bell v. Commissioner, 200 F.3d 545 (8th Cir.2000), "[t]axpayers have been litigating this theory for decades," taxpayer victories in these contests are few and far between. In *Bell* the taxpayer failed to establish that he was engaged in the trade or business of "buying, rehabilitating, and reselling corporations" because he did not provide any services to the distressed companies that might result in a return exceeding a typical investor's return and there was no pattern of sales indicating that profits on resale were attributable to taxpayer's work to rehabilitate corporations. There is something of a "Catch–22" in the taxpayer's situation in these cases. The courts are prone to state that to prove that he was in the trade or business of "buying, rehabilitating, and reselling corporations" the taxpayer must introduce evidence that the sales of the corporations occurred "in a manner that confirms that the taxpayer's profits were ... 'received directly for his own service' " or evidence of " 'an early and profitable sale' of the corporation." *Id.* The fact that a loan to the corporation has turned into a bad debt generally is factually inconsistent with either of these possibilities, unless the loan has continued to be outstanding for long after the sale.

CHAPTER 16

INTEREST AS A PROFIT–SEEKING EXPENSE

SECTION 1. DEDUCTIBLE INTEREST

Page 511:

After the carryover paragraph, insert:

The Tax Court's decision in *Redlark* was reversed by the Court of Appeals for the Ninth Circuit. 141 F.3d 936 (9th Cir.1998). The Court of Appeals reasoned that the words "properly allocable" in § 163(h)(2)(A), which excludes trade or business interest from the definition of nondeductible personal interest, were not intended to incorporate pre–1986 case law upon which the Tax Court relied. As have the other Courts of Appeals that have examined the issue, the Ninth Circuit found that the statutory language was ambiguous, and held that the Regulations were a reasonable interpretation of the statute and therefore valid. Accord Allen v. United States, 173 F.3d 533 (4th Cir.1999) (upholding the validity of Temp. Reg. § 1.163–9T(b)(2)(i)(A) with respect to interest on an income tax deficiency attributable to the income from a sole proprietorship); McDonnell v. United States, 180 F.3d 721 (6th Cir.1999) (same). Finally, in Robinson v. Commissioner, 119 T.C. 44 (2002), the Tax Court overruled its prior decision in *Redlark*, and followed the unanimous view of the Courts of Appeals that interest on a tax deficiency arising from the income of a sole proprietorship is nondeductible personal interest.

SECTION 2. WHAT IS INTEREST?

Page 521:

After the carryover paragraph, insert:

In Winn–Dixie Stores, Inc. v. Commissioner, 113 T.C. 254 (1999), aff'd, 254 F.3d 1313 (11th Cir.2001) (per curiam), the Tax Court applied the "economic substance" and sham transaction doctrines to deny an interest deduction. The taxpayer borrowed over $100,000,000 from an insurance company. The debt proceeds were used to purchase life insurance policies on approximately 36,000 of its employees and the policies were pledged to secure the loan. The plan and economic projections were quite complex, but the Tax Court compared the pre-tax and after-tax benefits to the taxpayer and concluded that because the predictable pre-tax costs of maintaining the plan exceeded the predictable pre-tax benefits, there was no nontax business purpose for the entire arrangement. Thus, since from an objective viewpoint the transaction was not likely to produce economic benefits apart from tax deductions, it lacked economic substance and the interest deduction was disallowed.

SECTION 3. STATUTORY LIMITATIONS ON THE INTEREST DEDUCTION

A. INVESTMENT INTEREST LIMITATION

Page 524:

After the third full paragraph, insert:

The 2003 Act added § 1(h)(11), which provides that dividends received by taxpayers other than corporations generally will be taxed at the same rate as long-term capital gains—15 percent for taxpayers otherwise taxable at a rate greater than 15 percent, and 5 percent for taxpayers otherwise at 10 or 15 percent (with a special 0 percent rate for 10 and 15 percent bracket taxpayers in 2008). See page 116. The existence of this preferential rate for dividends gives rise to tax arbitrage possibilities similar to those that arise when an interest deduction is allowed with respect to investments that produce only tax-favored capital gains, for which § 163(d) historically has limited interest deductions. Accordingly, the 2003 Act also amended § 163(d)(4) to exclude from the definition of net investment income any dividends that are taxed at preferential rates under § 1(h). However, §§ 1(h)(11)(D)(i) and 163(d)(4)(B) allow taxpayers to elect to forgo the preferential rates for dividends and to treat the dividends as investment income for purposes of § 163(d). If a taxpayer does not have other investment income against which investment interest may be deducted under § 163(d), it is to the taxpayer's advantage to elect not to have the preferential rates under § 1(h) apply to an amount of dividend income equal to the amount of investment interest that otherwise would be nondeductible by virtue of § 163(d).

CHAPTER 17

BUSINESS TAX CREDITS

SECTION 2. GENERAL BUSINESS CREDIT

Page 540:

At the end of the first paragraph, insert:

The § 51 work opportunity credit has been extended through December 31, 2002.

Page 541:

After the carryover sentence, insert:

The Tax Relief Extension Act of 1999 extended the increased research expenditures credit through June 30, 2004.

Page 544:

At the end of the first full paragraph, insert:

The renewable electric energy credit had been scheduled to expire after December 31, 2002. The life of the credit has been extended through December 31, 2004.

Page 545:

At the end of the first paragraph, insert:

The Indian employment credit has been extended through December 31, 2004.

After the first sentence of the third full paragraph, insert:

The hiring date for eligibility for the § 51A credit has been extended through December 31, 2003.

Page 549:

After the second full paragraph, insert:

O. EMPLOYER-PROVIDED CHILD CARE CREDIT

The 2001 Act added § 45F, which, starting in 2002, provides a credit of up to $150,000 to an employer for 25 percent of the employer's "qualified child care expenditures" and 10 percent of the employer's "qualified child care resource and referral expenditures." The credit is available with respect to a broad range of expenditures incurred to provide child care facilities and services for the taxpayer-employer's employees. Myriad special rules, worthy of any direct spending government subsidy program, are imposed on qualification for this tax expenditure, including a recapture of a credit if a facility ceases to used for child care after the credit is allowed with respect to the facility. In general, the benefits received by the employees as result of the expenses for which the employer receives the credit are excludable from gross income under § 129, discussed in the text at page 112.

PART IV

DUAL PURPOSE EXPENSES

CHAPTER 18

DEDUCTIBLE PROFIT-SEEKING EXPENSES VERSUS NONDEDUCTIBLE PERSONAL EXPENSES

SECTION 1. MEALS AND BUSINESS ENTERTAINMENT

B. STATUTORY LIMITATIONS

Page 558:

Replace the citations to the regulations with the following:

Sections 1.274–2(b)–(d); 1.274–5T(f)(2) and (3).

Page 558:

At the end of the fourth full paragraph, insert:

See Sutherland Lumber–Southwest, Inc. v. Commissioner, 114 T.C. 197 (2000), aff'd, 255 F.3d 495 (8th Cir.2001) (per curiam) (pursuant to § 274(e)(2), § 274 did not apply to an employer-corporation which provided private nonbusiness flights on a company owned airplane to employees because the fair market value of the flights was included in the employees' reported compensation; the employer's deduction was not limited to the lesser amount includable by the employees).

Page 563:

In the ninth and tenth lines of the first full paragraph, replace the citation to "Temp. Reg. § 1.274–5T(f)(4)" **with** "Treas. Reg. § 1.274–5(f)(4); see also Treas. Reg. § 1.62–2(e)(2)."

In the twelfth line of the first full paragraph, replace the citation to "Temp. Reg. § 1.274–5T(g), (j)" **with** "Treas. Reg. § 1.274–5(g), (j)."

Page 564:

At the end of the citation to Boyd Gaming Corp. v. Commissioner, insert:

, rev'd, 177 F.3d 1096 (9th Cir.1999) (because of the employer's requirement that all employees remain on the business premises throughout their shifts, more than one-half of employees received their meals for substantially noncompensatory business reasons and the convenience of the employer test was met; the "stay on the premises" rule standing alone was sufficient—the taxpayer was not required to show that the meals were linked to specific duties).

At the end of the carryover paragraph, insert:

The *Boyd Gaming Corp.* result was codified by the enactment in 1998 of § 119(b)(4), which provides that if more than one-half of the meals furnished to employees on an employer's business premises satisfy the "convenience of the employer test," then all meals furnished to all employees on those premises are deemed to have been provided for the convenience of the employer. The effect of this provision, in conjunction with the 1998 amendments to § 132(e)(2), is to assure that the employer may deduct the cost, and the employee may exclude from income the value, of all of the employees' meals as long as the employer can substantiate that more than half of them were for its convenience.

In Churchill Downs v. Commissioner, 307 F.3d 423 (6th Cir.2002), aff'g, 115 T.C. 279 (2000), the court held that § 274(n) limited Churchill Downs' deduction for the expenses of entertainment—the Kentucky Derby sport of Kings Gala, press receptions, hospitality tents, winners parties, etc.—in connection with the Kentucky Derby, the Breeders' Cup, and other major horse races to fifty percent of the cost. Although Churchill Downs was in the "entertainment business," the expenses for the functions were not part of its entertainment product, which was horse racing. The expenses were not deductible as the cost of entertainment available to the public under the exception in § 274(n)(2) and (e)(7), or as entertainment sold to customers under the exception in § 274(n)(2) and (e)(8), because the functions were by invitation only and were not open to the public.

SECTION 2. TRAVEL AND RELATED EXPENSES

Page 570:
After Revenue Ruling 94–47, insert:

Revenue Ruling 99–7

1999–1 C.B. 361.

ISSUE

Under what circumstances are daily transportation expenses incurred by a taxpayer in going between the taxpayer's residence and a work location deductible under § 162(a) of the Internal Revenue Code?

LAW AND ANALYSIS

Section 162(a) allows a deduction for all the ordinary and necessary expenses paid or incurred during the taxable year in carrying on any trade or business. Section 262, however, provides that no deduction is allowed for personal, living, or family expenses.

A taxpayer's costs of commuting between the taxpayer's residence and the taxpayer's place of business or employment generally are nondeductible personal expenses under §§ 1.162–2(e) and 1.262–1(b)(5) of the Income Tax Regulations. However, the costs of going between one business location and another business location generally are deductible under § 162(a). Rev. Rul. 55–109, 1955–1 C.B. 261.

Section 280A(c)(1)(A) (as amended by § 932 of the Taxpayer Relief Act of 1997, Pub. L. No. 105–34, 111 Stat. 881, effective for taxable years beginning after December 31, 1998) provides, in part, that a taxpayer may deduct expenses for the business use of the portion of the taxpayer's personal residence that is exclusively used on a regular basis as the principal place of business for any trade or business of the taxpayer. (In the case of an employee, however, such expenses are deductible only if the exclusive and regular use of the portion of the residence is for the convenience of the employer.) In Curphey v. Commissioner, 73 T.C. 766 (1980), the Tax Court held that daily transportation expenses incurred in going between an office in a taxpayer's residence and other work locations were deductible where the home office was the taxpayer's principal place of business within the meaning of § 280A(c)(1)(A) for the trade or business conducted by the taxpayer at those other work locations. The court stated that "[w]e see no reason why the rule that local transportation expenses incurred in travel between one business location and another are deductible should not be equally applicable *where the taxpayer's principal place of business with respect to the activities involved is his residence.*" 73 T.C. at

777–778 (emphasis in original). Implicit in the court's analysis in *Curphey* is that the deductibility of daily transportation expenses is determined on a business-by-business basis.

Rev. Rul. 190, 1953–2 C.B. 303, provides a limited exception to the general rule that the expenses of going between a taxpayer's residence and a work location are nondeductible commuting expenses. Rev. Rul. 190 deals with a taxpayer who lives and ordinarily works in a particular metropolitan area but who is not regularly employed at any specific work location. In such a case, the general rule is that daily transportation expenses are not deductible when paid or incurred by the taxpayer in going between the taxpayer's residence and a temporary work site inside that metropolitan area because that area is considered the taxpayer's regular place of business. However, Rev. Rul. 190 holds that daily transportation expenses are deductible business expenses when paid or incurred in going between the taxpayer's residence and a temporary work site outside that metropolitan area.

Rev. Rul. 90–23, 1990–1 C.B. 28, distinguishes Rev. Rul. 190 and holds, in part, that, for a taxpayer who has one or more regular places of business, daily transportation expenses paid or incurred in going between the taxpayer's residence and temporary work locations are deductible business expenses under § 162(a), regardless of the distance.

Rev. Rul. 94–47, 1994–2 C.B. 18, amplifies and clarifies Rev. Rul. 190 and Rev. Rul. 90–23, and provides several rules for determining whether daily transportation expenses are deductible business expenses under § 162(a). Under Rev. Rul. 94–47, a taxpayer generally may not deduct daily transportation expenses incurred in going between the taxpayer's residence and a work location. A taxpayer, however, may deduct daily transportation expenses incurred in going between the taxpayer's residence and a temporary work location outside the metropolitan area where the taxpayer lives and normally works. In addition, Rev. Rul. 94–47 clarifies Rev. Rul. 90–23 to provide that a taxpayer must have at least one regular place of business located "away from the taxpayer's residence" in order to deduct daily transportation expenses incurred in going between the taxpayer's residence and a temporary work location in the same trade or business, regardless of the distance. In this regard, Rev. Rul. 94–47 also states that the Service will not follow the decision in Walker v. Commissioner, 101 T.C. 537 (1993). Finally, Rev. Rul. 94–47 amplifies Rev. Rul. 190 and Rev. Rul. 90–23 to provide that, if the taxpayer's residence is the taxpayer's principal place of business within the meaning of § 280A(c)(1)(A), the taxpayer may deduct daily transportation expenses incurred in going between the taxpayer's residence and another work location in the same trade or business, regardless of whether the other work location is regular or temporary and regardless of the distance.

For purposes of both Rev. Rul. 90–23 and Rev. Rul. 94–47, a temporary work location is defined as any location at which the taxpayer performs services on an irregular or short-term (i.e., generally a matter of days or weeks) basis. However, for purposes of determining whether daily transportation expense allowances and per diem travel allowances for meal and lodging expenses are subject to income tax withholding under § 3402, Rev. Rul. 59–371, 1959–2 C.B. 236, provides a 1–year standard to determine whether a work location is temporary. Similarly, for purposes of determining the deductibility of travel away-from-home expenses under § 162(a)(2), Rev. Rul. 93–86, 1993–2 C.B. 71, generally provides a 1–year standard to determine whether a work location will be treated as temporary.

The Service has reconsidered the definition of a temporary work location in Rev. Rul. 90–23 and Rev. Rul. 94–47, and will replace the "irregular or short-term (i.e., generally a matter of days or weeks) basis" standard in those rulings with a 1-year standard similar to the rules set forth in Rev. Rul. 59–371 and Rev. Rul. 93–86.

If an office in the taxpayer's residence satisfies the principal place of business requirements of § 280A(c)(1)(A), then the residence is considered a business location for purposes of Rev. Rul. 90–23 or Rev. Rul. 94–47. In these circumstances, the daily transportation expenses incurred in going between the residence and other work locations in the same trade or business are ordinary and necessary business expenses (deductible under § 162(a)). See *Curphey*; see also Wisconsin Psychiatric Services v. Commissioner, 76 T.C. 839 (1981). In contrast, if an office in the taxpayer's residence does not satisfy the principal place of business requirements of § 280A(c)(1)(A), then the business activity there (if any) is not sufficient to overcome the inherently personal nature of the residence and the daily transportation expenses incurred in going between the residence and regular work locations. In these circumstances, the residence is not considered a business location for purposes of Rev. Rul. 90–23 or Rev. Rul. 94–47, and the daily transportation expenses incurred in going between the residence and regular work locations are personal expenses (nondeductible under §§ 1.162–2(e) and 1.262–1(b)(5)). See Green v. Commissioner, 59 T.C. 456 (1972) * * *.

For purposes of determining the deductibility of travel-away-from-home expenses under § 162(a)(2), Rev. Rul. 93–86 defines "home" as the "taxpayer's regular or principal (if more than one regular) place of business." See Daly v. Commissioner, 72 T.C. 190 (1979), aff'd, 662 F.2d 253 (4th Cir.1981); Commissioner v. Flowers, 326 U.S. 465 (1946), 1946–1 C.B. 57.

HOLDING

In general, daily transportation expenses incurred in going between a taxpayer's residence and a work location are nondeductible commuting expenses. However, such expenses are deductible under the circumstances described in paragraph (1), (2), or (3) below.

(1) A taxpayer may deduct daily transportation expenses incurred in going between the taxpayer's residence and a temporary work location

outside the metropolitan area where the taxpayer lives and normally works. However, unless paragraph (2) or (3) below applies, daily transportation expenses incurred in going between the taxpayer's residence and a temporary work location within that metropolitan area are nondeductible commuting expenses.

(2) If a taxpayer has one or more regular work locations away from the taxpayer's residence, the taxpayer may deduct daily transportation expenses incurred in going between the taxpayer's residence and a temporary work location in the same trade or business, regardless of the distance. (The Service will continue not to follow the Walker decision.)

(3) If a taxpayer's residence is the taxpayer's principal place of business within the meaning of § 280A(c)(1)(A), the taxpayer may deduct daily transportation expenses incurred in going between the residence and another work location in the same trade or business, regardless of whether the other work location is regular or temporary and regardless of the distance.

For purposes of paragraphs (1), (2), and (3), the following rules apply in determining whether a work location is temporary. If employment at a work location is realistically expected to last (and does in fact last) for 1 year or less, the employment is temporary in the absence of facts and circumstances indicating otherwise. If employment at a work location is realistically expected to last for more than 1 year or there is no realistic expectation that the employment will last for 1 year or less, the employment is not temporary, regardless of whether it actually exceeds 1 year. If employment at a work location initially is realistically expected to last for 1 year or less, but at some later date the employment is realistically expected to exceed 1 year, that employment will be treated as temporary (in the absence of facts and circumstances indicating otherwise) until the date that the taxpayer's realistic expectation changes, and will be treated as not temporary after that date.

The determination that a taxpayer's residence is the taxpayer's principal place of business within the meaning of § 280A(c)(1)(A) is not necessarily determinative of whether the residence is the taxpayer's tax home for other purposes, including the travel-away-from-home deduction under § 162(a)(2).

EFFECT ON OTHER DOCUMENTS

Rev. Rul. 190 and Rev. Rul. 59–371 are obsoleted. Rev. Rul. 90–23 and Rev. Rul. 94–47 are modified (regarding the definition of temporary work location) and superseded. * * *

Page 571:

After the carryover paragraph, insert:

For purposes of determining whether a work location within the metropolitan area in which the taxpayer lives is a "temporary" work location, which results in deductibility of expenses that otherwise would be nondeductible commuting expenses, a distinction must be drawn between a "temporary" work location with the meaning of Rev. Rul. 94–47, text page 567, and Rev. Rul. 99–7, page 73 of this supplement, and an "intermittent" but nonetheless regular work location. Rev. Rul. 90–23, 1990–1 C.B. 28, modified by Rev. Rul. 94–47, 1994–2 C.B. 18, modified and superceded (on other issues) by Rev. Rul. 99–7, 1999–1 C.B. 361, stated: "A taxpayer may be considered as working or performing services at a particular location on a regular basis whether or not the taxpayer works or performs services at that location every week or on a set schedule. Thus, for example, daily transportation expenses incurred by a doctor in going between the doctor's residence and one or more offices, clinics, or hospitals at which the doctor works or performs services on a regular basis are nondeductible commuting expenses." This principle has not been modified by subsequent Revenue Rulings.

Page 577:

After the carryover paragraph, insert:

In Strohmaier v. Commissioner, 113 T.C. 106 (1999), the Tax Court held that the "sleep or rest" rule requires a rest period of sufficient duration to require the securing of lodging. The court disallowed a deduction for meal expenses of an insurance agent who traveled between clients' locations and due to a medical condition was required to take long rest breaks during the day—usually in his automobile—which he claimed extended his work day and thus required that he eat meals on the road.

Page 582:

After the fifth full paragraph, insert:

In Johnson v. Commissioner, 115 T.C. 210 (2000), the taxpayer was the captain of a merchant ship that sailed worldwide. While on-board the vessel, he received lodging and meals excludable under § 119, but he paid for his other incidental travel expenses, for which he claimed a deduction. The Tax Court rejected the Commissioner's argument that the taxpayer was an itinerant with no tax home from which to be away, and held that his permanent residence, where he resided with his wife and their daughter, was his tax home. He had a legitimate reason for maintaining his personal residence while traveling throughout the world in the course of employment. The court's opinion stated as follows:

"According to [the Commissioner], an employee such as [the taxpayer] can never have a tax home because he continually travels to different cities during his employment. We disagree that such continual travel, in and of itself, serves to disqualify a taxpayer from having a tax home for purposes of section 162(a). Regardless of where a taxpayer performs most of his or her work, the fact that he or she maintains financially a fixed personal residence generally means that he or she has a tax home someplace."

SECTION 3. CLOTHING

Page 590:

At the end of the last paragraph, insert:

See also Genck v. Commissioner, T.C. Memo. 1998–105 (1998) (cost of jazz singer's stage clothes and makeup were deductible).

SECTION 5. "HOBBY LOSSES": IS THERE A PROFIT-SEEKING MOTIVE

Page 601:

At the end of the carryover paragraph, insert:

Under the multi-factor test set forth in the regulations, objective evidence of the manner in which the business is conducted is most important. On occasion, however, testimony from the taxpayer and the taxpayer's family regarding attitudes toward the activity is important. For example, in Novak v. Commissioner, T.C. Memo 2000–234, a physician whose Arabian horse breeding activity losses were disallowed, despite the fact that he was an expert in horse breeding and hired many experts, admitted that he became a doctor instead of a school teacher because while he was in college he father advised him, "if you ever want to have horses you can't be a school teacher, you've got to find a job where you can make some money, be a doctor or a dentist." Conversely, in Morley v. Commissioner, T.C. Memo. 1998–312, a dentist who engaged in Arabian horse breeding and sales was found to have a profit-seeking motive. The court noted as follows: "Mr. Morley's work on the farm was difficult, and it often precluded him from spending time with his family. Mrs. Morley credibly testified that she and her children missed her husband and that she would have preferred it if Mr. Morley had been at home instead of working on the horse-breeding activity. Mr. Morley arrived home after dark, very tired, in a bad mood, and dirty with a 'certain aroma' from his work on the farm. It appeared to the Court that Mrs. Morley resented the amount of time Mr. Morley spent on the horse-breeding activity and that she was unhappy that her husband came home every night dirty and smelly. We are not convinced that Mr. Morley would subject himself to such rigors solely for recreation or pleasure."

After the first full paragraph, insert:

In some cases the taxpayer's behavior makes the factual determination of whether there was an actual and honest profit objective almost too easy. O'Connell v. Commissioner, T.C. Memo. 2001–158, involved an insurance agent who avidly fished in billfish (e.g., marlin, and sailfish) tournaments. He owned and occasionally chartered out an ocean going fishing yacht that was used primarily for his sport fishing activities. Over seven years he lost approximately $1.4 million with respect to the yacht ownership activity. In disallowing the losses under § 183, the court quoted an interview the taxpayer gave for MARLIN magazine, in which he stated:

> You have to be in competitive offshore fishing for the sport * * * not the money. What you win could never cover the expenses. That's just a drop in the bucket! * * * If you're in tournament fishing for the money, you'll go broke. * * *
>
> In my mind, it is inconceivable to make any money at tournament fishing * * *. This is strictly a sport. If a guy only fished one or two tournaments in a year and he won one of them, then he might end up in the black for that year * * *. If you fish them a lot, though, it is really tough.

SECTION 6. MIXED USE PROPERTY

A. BUSINESS USE OF RESIDENCE

Page 610:

After the third full paragraph, insert:

Sengpiehl v. Commissioner, T.C. Memo. 1998–23, illustrates the difficult line-drawing questions that must be faced in applying § 280A. The taxpayer was a lawyer who worked exclusively from his home office. He carried the burden of proof that his living room was used exclusively as a conference room for his legal practice, even though it contained a piano, based on his credible testimony that he and his wife "usually did not entertain at home," their children "never had guests," and they used only the bedrooms, kitchen, bathroom, hallway, and occasionally the dining room, for personal purposes. No deduction was allowed with respect to the dining room, even though it was used exclusively for his legal practice during working hours, because it was occasionally used for family meals after working hours.

Page 613:

After the second full paragraph, insert:

Courts occasionally ameliorate the rigors of the *Soliman* test, text, page 611. For example, in Popov v. Commissioner, 246 F.3d 1190 (9th Cir.2001), the taxpayer was allowed a home office deduction for the portion of the rent on her one bedroom apartment (which she occupied with her husband and four-year-old daughter) attributable to the living room because the living room was used exclusively to practice the violin in connection with her work as a professional violinist for various orchestras and recording studios. On this basis, the court concluded that her living room was her principal place of business under the standards set forth in *Soliman*. The court reasoned that the "point of delivery" test does not apply to professional musicians because, quoting the German poet Heinrich Heine, "music stands 'halfway between thought and phenomenon, between spirit and matter, a sort of nebulous mediator, like and unlike each of the things it mediates—spirit that requires manifestation in time, and matter that can do without space.' " Since most of the taxpayer's time was spent practicing in her living room—where of course her four-year-old daughter *never ever* got underfoot—that was her principal place of business.

Page 617:

After the citation following the first full sentence of the third full paragraph, insert:

See Roy v. Commissioner, T.C. Memo. 1998–125 (1998) (§ 280A(g) does not provide an exclusion for *de minimis* amounts of income if rental period exceeds fourteen days; number of rental days is determinative, not amount of rental income).

B. VEHICLES, COMPUTERS, AND CELLULAR TELEPHONES

Page 619:

After the second full paragraph, insert:

Section 168(k), enacted in the 2001 Act, as amended by the 2003 Act, provides "bonus" first year depreciation for qualified property placed in service after September 10, 2001 and before May 6, 2003, and a deduction of fifty percent of the adjusted basis of qualified property placed in service after May 5, 2003 and before January 1, 2005. See page 61. Bonus depreciation is extended to passenger automobiles by increasing the § 280F(a)(1)(A)(i) limit by $4,600 for passenger automobiles that are qualified property placed in service after September 10, 2001 and before May 6, 2003, and by $7,650 for passenger automobiles that are qualified property placed in service after May 5, 2003 and before January 1, 2005.

CHAPTER 19

Expenditures Involving Both Personal and Capital Aspects

Section 1. Legal Expenses

Page 630:

At the end of the carryover paragraph, insert:

; Dana Corp. v. United States, 174 F.3d 1344 (Fed.Cir.1999) (legal fees paid by applying annual retainer against fees due in connection with purchase of corporate stock were capital expenses; origin of the claim test must be applied year-by-year based on the purpose for which the retainer is applied in that year—application in other years is not relevant; trial court erred in holding fee deductible because taxpayer corporation paid retainer to prevent law firm from representing any other corporation in an effort to takeover taxpayer and payment ordinarily provided no benefit beyond the year-end).

The determination of whether a profit-seeking expense is deductible under § 162 or, on the other hand, under § 212, and thereby subject to the myriad of more restrictive ancillary rules, turns on the "origin and character of the claim for which the expense was incurred and whether the claim bears a sufficient nexus to the taxpayer's business." Thus, for example, legal fees incurred by a sole proprietor or independent contractor to recover damages for conversion of business profits (and also any punitive damages awarded in addition to the compensatory damage) are deductible under § 162, but legal fees to recover taxable damages for personal defamation are deductible only under § 212. See Guill v. Commissioner, 112 T.C. 325 (1999).

Section 2. Expenses for Education and Seeking Employment

Page 644:

After the carryover paragraph, insert:

The 2001 Act added a special deduction for qualified tuition and related expenses in § 222. Section 222 operates completely independently of the rules of Treas. Reg. § 1.162–5 and is intended primarily to provide a deduction for parents who pay college tuition for their dependent children. The deduction is available to students who are not claimed as dependents by another taxpayer and pay their own tuition. See I.R.C. § 222(c)(3). The deduction is limited to tuition and related academic fees and does not extend to room and board. See I.R.C. § 222(d)(1), cross referencing to § 25A(g)(2). As is true with respect to the other tax expenditure provisions intended to subsidize higher education expenses, the deduction is not available for high-income taxpayers. Unlike most other tax expenditure benefits, which are phased-out over an income range, however, the § 222 deduction is subject to a cliff-effect disallowance rule. For 2002 and 2003, the maximum deduction is $3,000 for single taxpayers whose adjusted gross income does not exceed $65,000 and for married taxpayers filing a joint return whose gross income does not exceed $130,000. Taxpayers whose adjusted gross income exceeds those ceilings may not claim any deduction whatsoever. For 2004 and 2005, a maximum deduction of $4,000 is allowed for single taxpayer whose adjusted gross income does not exceed $65,000 and for married taxpayers filing a joint return whose gross income does not exceed $130,000. A maximum deduction of $2,000 is allowed for single taxpayers whose adjusted gross income does not exceed $80,000 and for married taxpayers filing a joint return whose gross income does not exceed $160,000. Taxpayers whose adjusted gross income exceeds the applicable $80,000 or $160,000 ceiling may not claim any deduction. Section 222(c) provides elaborate rules designed to deny the deduction if the taxpayer claims the § 25A HOPE scholarship or lifetime learning credit. Section 222(c) also reduces the deduction by any exclusions under § 135, text, page 344, § 529, text page 1214, or § 530, text, page 342. The § 222 deduction is allowed in reducing gross income to adjusted gross income; a taxpayer is not required to itemize deductions to claim the § 222 qualified tuition deduction. Section 222 sunsets completely after 2005.

PART V

Deductions and Credits for Personal Living Expenses

CHAPTER 20

Basic Exemptions, Standard Deduction, and Earned Income Credit

Section 1. Personal Exemptions and Standard Deduction

A. Personal Exemptions

Page 650:

After the fourth sentence of the third full paragraph, insert:

Miller v. Commissioner, 114 T.C. 184 (2000), held that a noncustodial father who had been allocated the dependency exemptions by a state court order, which had been signed by the taxpayer's former wife's attorney and a copy of which the taxpayer had attached to his tax return, was not entitled to claim the dependency exemptions with respect to his children because his former wife had not personally signed a waiver of her right to claim the exemptions.

Page 651:

After the carryover paragraph, insert:

The 2001 Act amended § 151 to phase-out over time the reduction of the amount allowable as personal exemptions under § 151(d) to increasingly lesser percentages—to 2/3 of the base formulaic reduction amount in 2006 and 2007 and 1/3 of the base formulaic reduction amount in 2008 and 2009. The reduction of personal exemptions is completely eliminated in 2010. See I.R.C. § 151(d) and (f). Like all of the amendments in the 2001 Act, however, these changes sunset on December 31, 2010. Thus, absent further congressional action § 151(d) would be revived in its current form in 2011.

B. STANDARD DEDUCTION, ITEMIZED DEDUCTIONS, AND THE ADJUSTED GROSS INCOME CONCEPT

Page 653:

After the fist full paragraph, insert:

The combined effect of the 2001 and 2003 Acts has been to increase the basic standard deduction amount for married taxpayers filing a joint return to twice the basic standard deduction amount for single individuals for 2003 and 2004. For 2005, the basic standard deduction amount for married taxpayers filing a joint return is 174 percent of the basic standard deduction for single individuals. This amount increases in steps over the following four years, with the result that in 2009 and thereafter the amount of the basic standard deduction for married taxpayers filing a joint return again will be twice the basic standard deduction for single individuals. However, these changes sunset on December 31, 2010.

Page 655:

After the second full paragraph, insert:

The 2001 Act amended § 68 to phase-out the reduction in itemized deductions to increasingly lesser percentages—to 2/3 of the base formulaic amount in 2006 and 2007 and 1/3 of the base formulaic amount in 2008 and 2009—before eliminating the operation of § 68 completely in 2010. See I.R.C. § 68(f) and (g). Like all of the amendments in the 2001 Act, however, these changes sunset on December 31, 2010. Thus, absent further congressional action § 68 would be revived in its current form in 2011.

SECTION 2. CREDITS FOR BASIC LIVING ALLOWANCES

A. THE CHILD CREDIT

Page 655:

After the first sentence of the last paragraph, insert:

As amended in the 2001 and 2003 Acts, the amount of the credit was increased to $600 for taxable years 2001 and 2002 and to $1,000 for 2003 and 2004. In 2005, the credit is reduced to $700, but then increases in steps to $1,000 for 2010. See I.R.C. § 24 (a)(2) However, these changes sunset on December 31, 2010. Thus, absent further congressional action the amount of the credit reverts to $500 in 2011.

Page 656:

After the third full paragraph, insert:

The 2001 Act amended § 24 to provide for partial refundablity of the child credit in 2001 through 2010. For 2001 through 2004, the credit is refundable to the extent of ten percent of the taxpayer's income in excess of $10,000 (indexed for inflation beginning in 2002). I.R.C. § 24(d)(1)(B)(i). For 2005 through 2010, the percentage increases to 15 percent. Section 24(d) continues to allow families with three or more children a refundable child credit equal to amount by which social security taxes exceed the sum of nonfundable credits and the earned income credit if that amount exceeds the amount otherwise refundable. I.R.C. § 24(d)(1)(B)(ii).

At the end of the last paragraph, insert:

The child credit has been amended to be creditable against both the regular tax and the alternative minimum tax. See I.R.C. § 24(b)(3).

B. EARNED INCOME CREDIT

Page 657:

After the last full paragraph, insert:

The 2001 Act made a number of changes in the earned income tax credit. First, the "modified gross income concept" in § 32(a)(2)(B), upon which the phase-out is based, was eliminated and the phase-out is based simply on adjusted gross income. This is a major simplification. Second, the "marriage penalty" imposed by triggering or accelerating the phase-out when an eligible taxpayer married and filed a joint return with a spouse who had income that affected the phase-out was mitigated somewhat by the addition of § 32(b)(2)(B), which provides higher thresholds for triggering the phase-out on joint returns than on single and head of household returns claiming the credit. Nevertheless, there remains a significant penalty on marriage by low income individuals eligible for the earned income tax credit. In addition, the "earned income" base for the credit is now limited to earned income that is included in gross income. I.R.C. § 32(c)(2)(A). Like all of the other provisions in the 2001 Act, however, these changes sunset on December 31, 2010.

The inflation-adjusted credit base and phase-out threshold for 2003 are set forth in Rev. Prov. 2002–70, § 3.06(1), 2002–46 I.R.B. 845:

Item	*Number of Qualifying Children*		
	One	Two or More	None
Earned Income Amount	$ 7,490	$10,510	$ 4,990
Maximum Credit	$ 2,547	$ 4,204	$ 382
Threshold Phase-out Amount	$13,730	$13,730	$ 6,240
Completed Phase-out Amount	$29,666	$33,692	$11,230
Threshold Phase-out Amount (Married Filing Jointly)	$14,730	$14,730	$ 7,250
Completed Phase-out Amount (Married Filing Jointly)	$30,666	$34,692	$12,230

Page 658:

At the end of the carryover paragraph, insert:

The 2001 Act simplified the definition of "qualifying child" by broadening the relationships that qualify. In addition to a child, grandchild, stepchild, or foster child, brothers, sisters, step brothers and sisters, and descendants of any of them can qualify if the taxpayer cares for the person as the taxpayer's own child. I.R.C. § 32(c)(3)(B).

At the end of the first full paragraph, insert:

Section 32(c)(1)(G), added in 1998, denies the earned income credit if the taxpayer fails to include the social security number of *every* child with respect to which the credit is claimed. This provision apparently is designed to discourage fraudulent claims of the credit. It is punitive in that it not only denies the credit with respect to a child for whom no social security number is included on the return, but is also denies the credit legitimately claimed with respect to one qualifying child if the taxpayer fraudulently claims the larger credit attributable to two qualifying children.

Pages 658–659:

Omit all of Illustrative Material item "B. Supplemental Child Credit."

Section 32(n) has been repealed.

CHAPTER 21

ITEMIZED PERSONAL DEDUCTIONS

SECTION 1. MEDICAL EXPENSES

Page 666:

After the first full paragraph of the *ILLUSTRATIVE MATERIAL*, insert:

It only took the Service 36 years to figure out that smoking kills. Based on 1988, 1990, 1994, and 1998 reports of the Surgeon General—the Service must have slept through the Surgeon General's famous 1963 report—in Rev. Rul. 99–28, 1999–1 C.B. 1269, the Service recognized that nicotine is a powerful addictive drug and that a strong causal link exists between smoking and several diseases. Accordingly, expenses incurred to participate in a smoking cessation program and to purchase prescription drugs to alleviate the effects of nicotine withdrawal were held to be deductible medical expenses even though the taxpayer had not been diagnosed as having any specific disease and even though participation in the program had not been suggested by a physician. The cost of nonprescription drugs purchased in connection with the program, however, is not a deductible medical expense. A few years later the Service woke up to the fact that obesity is an even greater American public health problem than smoking. Rev. Rul. 2002–19, 2002–16 I.R.B. 778, held that expenses for participating in a weight-loss program (e.g., meetings where participants develop a diet plan, receive diet menus and literature, and discuss problems encountered in dieting) are deductible as medical expenses under § 213 if the weight loss is prescribed to treat a disease, including obesity and hypertension (even if the taxpayer is not obese), diagnosed by a physician who has directed the taxpayer to lose weight. However, the ruling held that the cost of purchasing diet food items is not deductible.

Page 667:

At the end of the first full paragraph, insert:

See Rev. Rul. 2003–57, 2003–22 I.R.B. 959 (costs of breast reconstruction surgery following a mastectomy for cancer and costs of vision correction surgery are deductible medical care expenses; costs to whiten teeth discolored as a result of age are not medical care expenses under § 213(d) and are not deductible).

Page 671:

Omit the second full sentence and insert:

The deductible portion is 60 percent for 1999 through 2001, 70 percent for 2002, and 100 percent thereafter.

Page 673:

At the end of the third full paragraph, insert:

The deadline for establishing an MSA has been extended to 2003. Section 62(a)(18) was added by the 2001 Act to allow a deduction for contributions to an MSA by a taxpayer who does not itemize deductions.

SECTION 2. CHARITABLE CONTRIBUTIONS

Page 687:

After the fourth full paragraph, insert:

In Sklar v. Commissioner, 282 F.3d 610 (9th Cir.2002), the Court of Appeals for the Ninth Circuit upheld the denial of a deduction for tuition payments to a religious school that provided both religious and secular instruction, because taxpayers failed to prove that their payments for tuition exceeded the tuition charged by other private schools (i.e., the value of the secular education), citing United States v. American Bar Endowment, text, page 685.

Page 688:

At the end of the third full paragraph, insert:

Addis v. Commissioner, 118 T.C. 528 (2002), held that the substantiation requirements of § 170(f)(8) and Treas. Reg. § 1.170A–13(f)(7) are not met unless the charitable organization's estimate of the value of the benefits provided to the contributor was made in good faith.

Page 693:

At the end of the first full paragraph, insert:

The Tax and Trade Relief Extension Act of 1998 amended § 170(e)(5) to make the provision permanent.

Page 695:

In the eleventh line of the second full paragraph. After the citation to Rev. Rul. 88–37, insert:

Rev. Rul. 2003–28, 2003–11 I.R.B. 594 (a charitable contribution deduction is disallowed under § 170(f)(3) for a contribution of (1) a license to use a patent, if the taxpayer retains any substantial right in the patent (e.g., a right to license to others), or (2) a patent subject to a conditional reversion (e.g., a contribution of a patent to a university subject to a reversion if a particular faculty member ceases to be a member of the faculty within 15 years), unless the likelihood of the reversion is so remote as to be negligible; § 170(f)(3) does not bar a deduction for a contribution of a patent subject to a license or transfer restriction generally (e.g., a restriction of transfer or licensing for 3 years), but the restriction reduces what would otherwise be the value of the patent).

SECTION 3. STATE AND LOCAL TAXES

Page 703:

At the end of the second full paragraph, insert:

Treas. Reg. § 1.263A–2(a)(3)(ii) requires real estate developers to capitalize all real estate taxes paid with respect to any property if, at the time the taxes are incurred, it is reasonably likely that the property will be developed, even though no "production activities" of any sort have yet occurred. See Reichel v. Commissioner, 112 T.C. 14 (1999).

SECTION 4. QUALIFIED HOME MORTGAGE INTEREST AND QUALIFIED EDUCATION INTEREST

Page 715:

After the carryover paragraph, insert:

The 2001 Act amended § 221 in two significant respects. First, § 221(d), which limited the availability of the deduction to interest paid for the first sixty months of the loan repayment period, was repealed. Second, the phase-out range under § 221(b) was increased. For years after 2001, the deduction is phased out for single taxpayers whose "modified" adjusted gross income exceeds $50,000 and for married taxpayers filing a joint return whose modified gross income exceeds $100,000. The deduction is completely phased out for single taxpayers whose modified adjusted gross income exceeds $65,000 and for married taxpayers filing a joint return whose modified adjusted gross income exceeds $130,000. These phase-out thresholds continue to be indexed for inflation after 2001. See I.R.C. § 221(g).

In the second line of the first full paragraph, change "I.R.C. § 62(17)" to "I.R.C. § 62(a)(17)."

SECTION 5. CASUALTY LOSSES

Page 721:

At the end of the first paragraph of the *ILLUSTRATIVE MATERIAL*, insert:

In both Caan v. United States, 83 A.F.T.R.2d 99–1640 (C.D.Cal.1999) and Chamales v. Commissioner, T.C. Memo. 2000–033, the taxpayers, who were among O.J. Simpson's neighbors in the Brentwood section of Los Angeles, were denied casualty loss deductions for the diminution in value of their homes that they attributed to the murder of Nichole Brown Simpson and Ronald Goldman and the subsequent focus on O.J. Simpson as a suspect.

SECTION 6. TAX CREDITS FOR PERSONAL COSTS

Page 726:

After the last paragraph, insert:

Starting in 2003, the 2001 Act increased the § 21 dependent care credit percentage to 35 percent of eligible expenses. The Act also increased the ceiling amount of employment-related expenses that qualify for the credit to $3,000 if there is only one qualifying individual or $6,000 if there are two or more qualifying individuals in the household. The maximum dependent care credit thus is $1,050 in the case of one qualifying individual and $2,100 in the case of two or more qualifying individuals. Under the 2001 Act, the reduction in the credit begins at $15,000 of adjusted gross income rather than $10,000. Thus, a taxpayer with more than $38,000 of adjusted gross income is entitled to a credit of only 20 percent of employment-related qualifying expenses. Like all of the amendments in the 2001 Act, however, these changes sunset on December 31, 2010.

Page 729:

At the end of the third full paragraph, insert:

The 2001 made the § 23 adoption credit a "permanent" provision, subject to sunset after 2010 like all of the other provisions of the 2001 Act. In addition, the 2001 Act increased the ceiling on the credit to $10,000, subject to an annual inflation adjustment. Starting in 2003, a $10,000 (as adjusted for inflation) credit is allowed with respect to the adoption of a "special needs" child even if no qualified adoption expenses have been incurred. I.R.C. § 23(a)(1)(B).

Page 730:

At the end of the carryover paragraph, insert:

The 2001 Act amended § 23(b)(2) to begin the phase-out of the adoption credit at an adjusted gross income of $150,000, subject to an annual inflation adjustment. Apart from the inflation adjustment, it is now completely phased out when adjusted gross income exceeds $190,000.

Page 730:

At the end of the second full paragraph, insert:

No credit is allowed under § 25A for any amounts paid for tuition that are taken into account in determining the amount of an excludable distribution from an educational investment account under § 530, discussed at page 342 of the text.

*

PART VI

TAXATION OF PROPERTY TRANSACTIONS

CHAPTER 22

THE ROLE OF DEBT IN PROPERTY TRANSACTIONS

SECTION 2. ACQUISITIONS AND DISPOSITIONS: DEBT IN BASIS AND AMOUNT REALIZED

Page 754:

After the last paragraph, insert:

But where recourse debt is involved the results might be different. Frazier v. Commissioner, 111 T.C. 243 (1998), held that if a mortgagee bids-in property at an arbitrary amount at a foreclosure sale, the mortgagor-taxpayer is entitled to establish the fair market value of the property by extrinsic evidence. In that event, the sales price, and thus the amount realized on the sale of the property, is not the bid price, but is the fair market value of the property, which may be lower than the bid price. The amount by which the discharged recourse mortgage debt exceeds the fair market value then is cancellation of indebtedness income, discussed at page 282 of the text, which might be excludable under § 108(a)(1)(B) if the taxpayer is insolvent.

CHAPTER 23

DEFERRED RECOGNITION OF GAIN ON DISPOSITIONS OF PROPERTY

SECTION 1. LIKE-KIND EXCHANGES

Page 780:

After the carryover paragraph, insert:

Wiechens v. United States, 228 F.Supp.2d 1080 (D.Ariz.2002), held that an exchange of water rights for a limited quantity of water for a duration of 50 years, which under state law were real property, for a fee simple interest in land did not qualify for nonrecognition under § 1031. The water rights and a fee simple interest in land were not "like-kind," even under the broad standard of Reg. § 1.1031(a)–1(b). The court rejected the taxpayer's argument that the 50–year water rights were analogous to the 30–year lease that qualified as like-kind with a fee simple in real estate under Treas. Reg. § 1.1031(a)–1(c). Because the water rights were not perpetual, they were not like-kind with a fee simple under Rev. Rul. 55–749, 1955–2 C.B. 295, text, page 780.

Page 782:

After the second full paragraph, insert:

Rev. Rul. 2002–83, 2002–49 I.R.B. 927, applied § 1031(f) in the following circumstances. Individual A owned highly appreciated real property held for investment (Property 1) and individual B, who was related to individual A, owned real property (Property 2), which was not appreciated. In a multi-party like-kind exchange, A and B each transferred their properties to an unrelated qualified intermediary, and C, an unrelated purchaser of Property 1, transferred cash to the qualified intermediary, who transferred Property 1 to C, Property 2 to A, and the cash to B. The ruling held § 1031(f) applied to deny nonrecognition to a taxpayer—A—who transfers relinquished property to a qualified intermediary in exchange for replacement property formerly owned by a related party if, as part of the transaction, the related party receives cash or other non-like-kind property for the replacement property. The legislative history of § 1031(f), H.R. Rep. No. 247, 101st Cong. 1st Sess. 1340 (1989), indicates that the purpose of the provision is to deny nonrecognition treatment for transactions in which related parties make like-kind exchanges of high basis property for low basis property in anticipation of the sale of the low basis property. Accordingly, § 1031(f)(4) applied because the multi-party exchange "was part of a transaction (or a series of transactions) structured to avoid the purposes of § 1031(f)(1)."

Page 791:

In the thirteenth and fourteenth lines of the first full paragraph, change "Treas. Reg. § 1.1031(k)–1(f)(2)–(4)" **to** "Treas. Reg. § 1.1031(k)–1(g)(2)–(4)".

In the fourteenth line of the first full paragraph, change "Treas. Reg. § 1.1031(k)–1(f)(6)" **to** "Treas. Reg. § 1.1031(k)–1(g)(6)".

In the first line of the second full paragraph, change "Treas. Reg. § 1.1031(k)–1(f)(6)" **to** "Treas. Reg. § 1.1031(k)–1(g)(6)".

Page 791:

After the second full paragraph, insert:

C. REVERSE DEFERRED EXCHANGES

On some occasions a taxpayer who wishes to engage in a like-kind exchange from a tax-planning viewpoint locates the property that the taxpayer wishes to acquire before locating another party to acquire the property that the taxpayer plans to relinquish. The case law has recognized that § 1031 can apply when a taxpayer receives replacement property before transferring the relinquished property. In Rutherford v. Commissioner, T.C. Memo 1978–505, the taxpayer-farmer entered into an agreement with another farmer under which the other farmer would transfer twelve half-blood heifers to the taxpayer, who would have the heifers artificially inseminated at his expense. The taxpayer, in exchange, would transfer to the other farmer the first twelve three-quarter-blood heifers born as a result of the artificial insemination. The taxpayer received the half-blood heifers in 1973 and satisfied his obligation by delivering the three-quarter-blood heifers to the other farmer over a period beginning in 1975 and ending in 1977. The Tax Court held that the taxpayer had engaged in a § 1031 like-kind exchange by his transfer of the relinquished property (the three-quarter blood heifers) for the replacement property (the half-blood heifers). In this "reverse exchange," the taxpayer received the replacement property before the relinquished property even existed.

A number of cases have involved exchanges of real estate in somewhat similar, but more complex transactions. In J.H. Baird Publishing Co. v. Commissioner, 39 T.C. 608 (1962) (acq.) and Coastal Terminals Inc. v. United States, 320 F.2d 333 (4th Cir.1963), the courts found a like-kind exchange to have occurred where, at the taxpayer's direction, the replacement property was acquired by a third party who proceeded to make significant improvements. After completion of the taxpayer-directed construction, the newly constructed property was acquired by the taxpayer as replacement property in exchange for the relinquished property. Biggs v. Commissioner, 632 F.2d 1171 (5th Cir.1980), text, page 788, reached a similar result on analogous facts. In all of these cases, however, the courts found that the third-party was acting as a principal, not as the taxpayer's agent, in acquiring and improving the property, even though the acquisition and improvement were pursuant to an agreement between the taxpayer and the third party. Thus, in form, if not in substance, the exchanges were simultaneous rather than reverse deferred exchanges.

Neither § 1032(a)(3) nor Treas. Reg. § 1.1031(k)–1. deal with reverse deferred exchanges. The juxtaposition of the *Rutherford* case and the cases involving real estate raises the question of the extent to which the taxpayer can "park" property with a third party who will improve the property to the taxpayer's specifications, possibly with financing provided by the taxpayer, and still have the entire transaction treated as a like-kind exchange. Rather than develop the parameters of permissible "parking" arrangements in reverse deferred like-kind exchanges by litigation and regulations, the Internal Revenue Service issued a safe-harbor revenue procedure. Rev. Proc. 2000–37, 2000–2 C.B. 308, provides like-kind exchange treatment for "parking" reverse deferred exchanges when the replacement property is received by an "exchange accommodation titleholder" (EAT) before the taxpayer transfers the relinquished property. Under the revenue procedure, the EAT will be treated as the owner of the property if the property is held in a "Qualified Exchange Accommodation Arrangement" (QEAA). The EAT must hold either legal or beneficial title to the property, termed "qualified indicia of ownership." The EAT and the taxpayer must enter into a QEAA in writing within five days of the EAT acquiring qualified indicia of ownership of the replacement property, the relinquished property must be identified (consistently with the rules of § 1031(a)(3) and Treas. Reg. § 1.1031(k)–1(g)(4)) within 45 days of the EAT acquiring qualified indicia of ownership to the replacement property, and the exchange must be completed within 180 days of the EAT acquiring the qualified indicia of ownership. The taxpayer may guarantee any debt incurred by the EAT to improve the property, advance funds to the EAT to pay the purchase price, lease the property from the accommodation party, supervise the property or construction, and protect the accommodation party against risk of loss from fluctuations in value. An EAT may, but need not, be a qualified intermediary (as defined in Treas. Reg. § 1.1031(k)–1(g)(4)), but may not be a disqualified party (as defined in Treas. Reg. § 1.1031(k)–1(k)). If the EAT holds both properties simultaneously for a period not in excess of 180 days and the EAT is a qualified intermediary, the transaction can qualify under both the revenue procedure safe harbor and § 1031(a)(3).

Outside of the safe harbor of Rev. Proc. 2000–37, however, reverse deferred like-kind exchanges will not qualify if not structured correctly. In DeCleene v. Commissioner, 115 T.C. 457 (2000), the taxpayer purchased a parcel of land which he wanted to improve and use to replace in his business a property that he wanted to relinquish. The taxpayer located a buyer for the property he wanted to relinquish and entered into the following plan. The taxpayer sold the recently purchased replacement property to the buyer at a price equal to its adjusted basis, with payment deferred. The buyer held the property while a new building, financed by the taxpayer, was constructed on it, and then transferred it to the taxpayer in exchange for the relinquished property. The taxpayer claimed that the transaction was a direct reverse exchange, without the participation of any accommodation party, but the Tax Court held that there was a taxable sale of property, not a like-kind exchange. The buyer had never acquired the benefits and burdens of ownership of the replacement property because the taxpayer and the buyer had agreed at the outset that relinquished property and the replacement property were of equal value. The court held that *Bloomington Coca–Cola Bottling Co. v. Commissioner*, 189 F.2d 14 (7th Cir.1951), which held that no § 1031 exchange occurs when a taxpayer constructs a building on property he already owns, was indistinguishable.

SECTION 2. INVOLUNTARY CONVERSIONS

Page 792:
After the second full paragraph, insert:

Willamette Industries, Inc. v. Commissioner

United States Tax Court, 2002.
118 T.C. 126.

OPINION

■ Gerber, J.

* * * The parties filed cross-motions for partial summary judgment. The controversy concerns whether petitioner is entitled to defer gain resulting from the salvage (processing and sale) of damaged trees under section 1033. The parties have agreed on the salient facts. The controverted issue involves a legal question that is ripe for summary judgment.

Background

Petitioner is an Oregon corporation with its principal office in Portland, Oregon. Petitioner operates a vertically integrated forest products manufacturing business, which includes the ownership and processing of trees (raw materials) at various types of manufacturing plants, including lumber mills, plywood plants, and paper mills. The raw materials used in the manufacturing process are derived from petitioner's trees and from trees grown by others. Approximately 40 percent of petitioner's timber needs is acquired from petitioner's timberland, which comprises 1,253,000 acres of forested land.

Petitioner suffered damage to some of its standing trees during each of the years in issue, 1992–95. The damage was caused by wind, ice storms, wildfires, or insect infestations. The damage left part of petitioner's damaged trees standing and part of them fallen. The intended use of the trees was continued growth and cultivation until maturity, at which time the trees would have been systematically and efficiently harvested. The damage occurred prior to the intended time for harvest.

Petitioner salvaged its damaged trees to avoid further loss (from decay, insects, etc.) by means of the following steps: (1) Taking down damaged trees that remained standing; (2) cutting damaged trees into standard length logs; (3) stripping the branches from the logs; (4) dragging the logs to a pickup point; (5) grading and sorting the logs; (6) stacking the logs at a landing point; and (7) loading the logs onto trucks for further use or processing.

Petitioner chose to take the seven steps described in the preceding paragraph, rather than attempting to sell the damaged trees in place to a third party. Once it performed the seven steps, its options were to (1) attempt to sell the partially processed damaged trees to a third party; or (2) complete the processing of the damaged trees in its own plants in the ordinary course of its business. Petitioner chose the latter and completed the processing itself.

Petitioner relies on section 1033 for involuntary conversion treatment (deferral of gain). Petitioner did not realize income from harvesting and processing the damaged trees until it sold the products it manufactured from the damaged trees. Petitioner is seeking to defer only that portion of the gain attributable to the difference between its basis and the fair market value of the damaged trees as of the time its salvage of them began; that is, the value petitioner contends would have been recognized if it had sold the damaged trees on the open market instead of further processing and/or milling the damaged trees into finished products. Petitioner further contends that it is not attempting to defer any portion of the gain attributable to the processing, milling, or finishing of products.[5] Respondent determined that petitioner understated income by improperly deferring gain from the

5. Based on a hypothetical example presented by petitioner, the majority of the gain deferred would appear to be attributable to the difference between the fair market value of the damaged trees and petitioner's basis. Petitioner posed a hypothetical example which included the premises that the damaged trees had a $100 basis and a $475 selling price if sold in place. If the damaged trees were processed into logs, the processing cost would be $25 resulting in a $500 selling price. Petitioner further posits that the cost of milling timber is $100 and that a finished product would have a $610 selling price, resulting in $10 of gain from milling. Petitioner argues that, under this hypothetical, respondent would have allowed a deferral of the $375 gain if petitioner had sold the damaged trees in place. Petitioner contends that respondent has denied any deferral whatsoever, even though the milling of timber into a final product adds only $10 of additional gain in the context of petitioner's hypothetical. We consider here only whether petitioner is entitled to use sec. 1033. The parties have left to another day the question of the amount of gain to be deferred if petitioner's motion for partial summary judgment is granted. See *infra* note 6.

sale of the end product of the damaged trees, as follows: 1992—$647,953; 1993—$2,276,282; 1994—$3,592,035; and 1995—$4,831,462.

Discussion

The specific question we consider is whether petitioner is disqualified from electing deferral of gain under section 1033 because it processed damaged trees into end or finished products rather than being compelled simply to sell the damaged trees.[6]

Respondent contends that under section 1033 the realization of gain must stem directly or solely from the damage and the involuntary conversion. More particularly, respondent asserts that petitioner's conversion was not "involuntary" because damaged trees were processed into end products in the ordinary course of its business. Respondent points out that section 1033 is a relief provision which does not or should not include petitioner's situation; i.e., where the damaged trees are processed in the same manner as undamaged trees. Finally, respondent contends that section 1033 was not intended for the long-term deferral of profits from petitioner's timber processing and manufacturing business.[7]

Petitioner argues that its factual situation complies literally with the requirements of section 1033 allowing deferral of gain realized from salvaging its damaged trees. Specifically, petitioner contends that it was compelled (in order to avoid further damage or loss) to salvage (process) the damaged trees resulting in an involuntary conversion within the meaning of section 1033. Petitioner also points out that the conversion was "involuntary" because the damaged trees were not scheduled for harvest at the time of the damage. In response to respondent's argument, petitioner contends that its choices for salvaging the damaged trees should not preclude deferral of the portion of the gain that it was compelled to realize on account of the damage to its trees. Petitioner emphasizes that it is not attempting to defer gain from processing and/or milling the damaged trees. Petitioner seeks to defer only that portion of the gain attributable to the difference between its basis in the damaged trees and their fair market value at the time the process of salvaging the trees began.

Section 1033 provides, under certain prescribed circumstances, for relief from taxpayer's gains realized from involuntary conversion of proper-

6. The parties have isolated this issue from other unresolved issues, including petitioner's substantiation of the quantity and value of the damaged trees; the amount of gain realized from sale of damaged trees; the amount of gain that may be deferred; and the determination of the correct year(s) for deferring the gain.

7. Respondent's contention appears to address the possibility that petitioner reinvested the proceeds (and deferred gains) from the sale of the damaged trees in replacement property in the form of relatively young trees, thereby resulting in lengthy deferral of the subject gains. Respondent's contention, however, is more properly directed at the question of whether petitioner reinvested the proceeds in qualified replacement property, a question which is not at issue in the cross-motions for partial summary judgment.

ty. The relief provided for under section 1033 is deferral of the gain from involuntary conversion, so long as the proceeds are used to acquire qualified replacement property.

The purpose of section 1033 was described, as follows:

> The purpose of the statute is to relieve the taxpayer of unanticipated tax liability arising from involuntary * * * [conversion] of his property, by freeing him from such liability to the extent that he re-establishes his prior commitment of capital within the period provided by the statute. The statute is to be liberally construed to accomplish this purpose. On the other hand, it was not intended to confer a gratuitous benefit upon the taxpayer by permitting him to utilize the involuntary interruption in the continuity of his investment to alter the nature of that investment tax free. * * *

Filippini v. United States, 318 F.2d 841, 844 (9th Cir.1963).

The earliest predecessor of section 1033 was section 214(a)(12) of the Revenue Act of 1921, ch. 136, 42 Stat. 227 (1921 Act). Except for certain modifications not pertinent to the question we consider, the purpose and substance of section 214(a)(12) of the 1921 Act was the same as the version of section 1033 under consideration in this case.

Only a limited amount of legislative history has accompanied the enactment of the various involuntary conversion relief provisions since 1921. The House and Senate reports issued in connection with section 214(a)(12) of the 1921 Act explained that the relief "permits the taxpayer to omit or deduct the gains involuntarily realized, when he proceeds forthwith in good faith to invest the proceeds of such conversion in the acquisition of similar property or in establishment of a replacement fund therefor." H. Rept. 350, 67th Cong., 1st Sess. 12 (1921), 1939–1 C.B. (Part 2) 168, 177; accord S. Rept. 275, 67th Cong., 1st Sess. 15 (1921), 1939–1 C.B. (Part 2) 181, 191.

From that limited legislative history, it can be gleaned that Congress intended relief from involuntary conversions only to the extent of the "proceeds of such conversion", and expected taxpayers to acquire replacement property within a reasonable time. Obviously, relief was intended only where the conversion was involuntary. Although Congress was concerned about the timeliness and "good faith" of efforts in seeking replacement property, there was no explanation or particular focus upon the use of damaged assets in the taxpayer's business.

Where the complete destruction or loss of property has occurred, there has been only a limited amount of litigation about whether a taxpayer should be allowed to defer the attendant gain. Where the destruction or loss to property is partial, however, additional questions have arisen.

In C.G. Willis, Inc. v. Commissioner, 41 T.C. 468 (1964), affd. 342 F.2d 996 (3d Cir.1965), the taxpayer's ship was damaged in a 1957 collision, and the insurance company paid $100,000 to the taxpayer. The insurance payment was approximately $9,000 less than the taxpayer's basis in the ship, and, accordingly, no gain was realized for 1957. In 1958, however, the taxpayer sold the damaged, but unrepaired, ship for an amount which exceeded the remaining basis by approximately $86,000. Under those circumstances, it was held that the 1958 sale was not an "involuntary conversion" within the meaning of section 1033 so that the gain had to be recognized and could not be deferred. In so holding, it was explained that the damage to the taxpayer's ship was insufficient to compel the taxpayer to sell and, accordingly, the sale was not involuntary. Id. at 476. In that setting, "involuntary conversion" under section 1033 was defined to mean "that the taxpayer's property, through some outside force or agency beyond his control, is no longer useful or available to him for his purposes." Id.; see also Wheeler v. Commissioner, 58 T.C. 459, 462–463 (1972) (where it was held that the taxpayer's choice to destroy his building was not an involuntary conversion).

In S.H. Kress & Co. v. Commissioner, 40 T.C. 142 (1963), we held that condemnation of the taxpayer's property was imminent and unavoidable, and that the only realistic alternatives were to either await condemnation or to sell to an appropriate buyer. We found that those circumstances met the "compulsorily or involuntarily converted" requirement of section 1033, (citing Masser v. Commissioner, 30 T.C. 741 (1958)). Accordingly, even though a taxpayer has choices or alternatives a disposition may be deemed involuntary so that section 1033 relief remains available.

Masser v. Commissioner, supra, involved section 112(f)(1) of the Internal Revenue Code of 1939 (another predecessor of section 1033). In *Masser,* the taxpayer operated an interstate trucking business from two proximately positioned pieces of business realty that were used as part of a single economic unit. One of the properties was subject to imminent condemnation, but the taxpayer sold both parcels. In that circumstance, we held that both pieces of realty were involuntarily converted and the gain from both could be deferred.

Those cases reveal two general elements as being necessary to qualify for deferral of gain under section 1033. First, a taxpayer's property must be involuntarily damaged, and second the property must no longer be available for the taxpayer's intended business purposes for the property.

The Commissioner issued a revenue ruling that specifically focused on whether gain from the sale of trees damaged by a hurricane qualified under section 1033. In that ruling it was held that the gain on sale of uprooted trees was "voluntary" and, in addition, that there was no direct conversion into money in the circumstances expressed in the ruling. See Rev. Rul. 72–372, 1972–2 C.B. 471. The principal rationale for the holding of Rev. Rul. 72–372, supra, was that the hurricane did not cause the conversion of the trees into cash or other property directly resulting in gain from the damage.

In a second ruling, however, the 1972 ruling was revoked. See Rev. Rul. 80–175, 1980–2 C.B. 230. The 1980 ruling permitted deferral of gain from the sale of damaged trees. The factual predicate for both rulings was as follows:

> the taxpayer was the owner of timberland. As a result of a hurricane, a considerable number of trees were uprooted. The timber was not insured, and once downed, was subject to decay or being rendered totally worthless by insects within a relatively short period of time. The taxpayer was, however, able to sell the damaged timber and realized a gain from such sale. The proceeds of the sale were used to purchase other standing timber.

The rationale articulated in Rev. Rul. 80–175, supra, is that gain is "postponed on the theory that the taxpayer was compelled to dispose of property and had no economic choice in the matter" and that the taxpayer "was compelled by the destruction of the timber to sell it for whatever the taxpayer could or suffer a total loss." Id., 1980–2 C.B. at 231. Accordingly, the taxpayer in the 1980 ruling was found to have met the two part test; i.e., that the damage was involuntary and the timber was no longer available for the taxpayer's intended business purpose. Most significantly, the 1980 ruling eliminated the requirement that the damage-causing event convert the property directly into cash or other property.

The 1980 ruling also contained a comparison with the holding in C.G. Willis, Inc. v. Commissioner, supra, as follows:

> In the present case, the downed timber was not repairable and was generally no longer useful to the taxpayer in the context of its original objective. The destruction caused by the hurricane forced the taxpayer to sell the downed timber for whatever price it could get. Unlike the situation in *Willis*, the sale of the downed timber was dictated by the damage caused by the hurricane. [Rev. Rul. 80–175, supra, 1980–2 C.B. at 232.]

The taxpayer in the 1980 ruling apparently intended to grow trees and/or hold timberland for sale at a particular maturity. The hurricane caused the taxpayer to involuntarily sell/use the trees prior to the time intended for harvest or sale. The taxpayer's intended purpose or use was only affected as to timing, and the sale was prior to the time the taxpayer intended to sell or harvest.

Returning to the disagreement here, petitioner contends that, at the time of the damage, it did not intend to harvest the damaged trees, so that the conversion was involuntary and within the meaning of the statute. Petitioner argues that a taxpayer may not have a choice as to *whether* to dispose of damaged property, but a taxpayer may have a choice as to *how* to dispose of damaged property.

Respondent contends that petitioner should not be entitled to such deferral because of its choice to further process the trees into logs or finished products, its original intention. Respondent's position in this case is a reversion to the requirement of the 1972 ruling that the sale (conversion to cash) be the direct result of the damage-causing event. For more than 21 years, the Commissioner's ruling position has permitted section 1033 deferral even though the conversion is not directly into cash.

Petitioner in this case is effectively no different from the taxpayer in the 1980 ruling.[11] Petitioner's conversion was involuntary, and petitioner was forced to act or suffer complete loss of the damaged trees. Section 1033 could be interpreted to permit either a direct or an indirect conversion. The case law permits indirect conversion, but the Commissioner's 1972 ruling denied relief because the trees damaged by the hurricane were sold by the taxpayer. The Commissioner, in revoking the 1972 ruling has permitted, since 1980, section 1033 relief where there is a sale (a voluntary act) of the damaged property. Respondent has denied relief here because petitioner processed rather than sold the damaged trees.

The critical factor is that petitioner was compelled to harvest the damaged trees prior to the time it had intended. The possibility that the partial damage to petitioner's trees might have been relatively small or resulted in a nominal amount of reduction in gain is not a reason to deny relief. In addition, if petitioner's salvage efforts were more successful than other taxpayers that is not a reason for denial of relief under section 1033.

Petitioner's circumstances fulfill the statutory purpose and intent. There was unanticipated tax liability due to various casualties that damaged the trees. Petitioner seeks to defer the gain that was occasioned by the damage and which it had reinvested in like property. Petitioner had not planned to harvest the damaged trees. Identical to the taxpayer's situation in the 1980 ruling, petitioner's trees were damaged by forces without its control, and petitioner was compelled to salvage its damaged trees prior to the intended date for harvest, sale, and/or processing into end products. Unlike the taxpayer in C.G. Willis v. Commissioner, supra, petitioner was forced to salvage (process or sell) the damaged trees or suffer a total loss.

Respondent's attempt to distinguish petitioner's situation from the ruling does not reconcile with the rationale of the 1980 ruling, the underlying statute, and case law. The taxpayer in the ruling and petitioner were both forced to salvage the damaged trees or suffer the imminent and total loss of the damaged trees. The taxpayer in the ruling and petitioner were prematurely forced to salvage (sell or use) the damaged trees. The damaged trees were used in their businesses, but not in the same manner as they would normally have done. In the 1980 ruling, the taxpayer was forced to sell the trees under unintended business conditions. Likewise, petitioner was forced to use the damaged trees, albeit in its manufacturing process,

11. Respondent has not argued that the 1980 ruling was not in accord with sec. 1033 or the case law. Respondent's position in this case, however, does not comport with the outcome or reasoning of the 1980 ruling.

under unintended business conditions; i.e. before maturity and/or before the time at which the trees would normally be ready for efficient harvest.

Respondent also argues that petitioner is not entitled to defer gain because "there were no actual sales of damaged timber." Respondent argues that section 1033 requires a sale or conversion of the damaged property into money or property similar in use to the damaged property. Section 1033 simply requires that property be involuntarily converted into money or property. There is no requirement, as argued by respondent, that the deferred gain be derived in a particular manner; i.e., only from a distress sale. Based on the holding of Rev. Rul. 80–175, 1980–2 C.B. 230, it is unlikely that respondent would have questioned the deferral of gain if petitioner had been forced to sell the damaged trees in place.[12]

Finally, respondent contends that section 1033 was intended to provide relief for taxpayers who experience "destruction [of property] in whole or in part". Although respondent agrees that petitioner had a casualty, damage to the trees, and petitioner was compelled to salvage them, respondent infers that petitioner's situation is somehow not directly affected by the destruction. Respondent contends that petitioner's gain is voluntary or not caused by the damage because petitioner is able to process the logs into finished products.

Admittedly, petitioner's circumstances may appear more favorable than might have been expected after a "casualty", but the statute does not have a quantitative threshold. Petitioner is not seeking a windfall in the form of the deferral of gain from processing and/or making the finished products. Nor is petitioner attempting to "utilize the involuntary interruption in the continuity of his investment to alter the nature of that investment tax free." Filippini v. United States, 318 F.2d at 844. Petitioner is seeking to defer the unexpected gain that resided in trees that it had not, at the time of the damage, intended to harvest and to reinvest that gain in trees that will fulfill petitioner's intended purpose.[13] Such deferral was the intended purpose for the enactment of section 1033.

Respondent argues that the purpose of section 1033 may be better served where a taxpayer is unable to process damaged property into the taxpayer's usual product(s). But that disability is not a threshold for relief or a requirement of the statute. Section 1033 is a relief provision, and we are to construe it liberally to effect its purpose. Davis v. United States, 589

12. If we were to approve respondent's approach, taxpayers, who were unable to sell damaged assets without some additional processing would be denied sec. 1033 relief. That distinction could not have been intended and certainly was not expressed in the legislation.

13. Contrary to the import of respondent's argument, petitioner did not intend to harvest trees that happen to become diseased or damaged. Petitioner intended to efficiently and systematically harvest trees and to maximize its profit. It was not petitioner's intent to randomly cull and process trees that happened to become damaged.

F.2d 446, 450 (9th Cir.1979); Asjes v. Commissioner, 74 T.C. 1005, 1014 (1980).

Respondent would have this Court impose its own judgment as to which taxpayer deserves relief. So, for example, if a taxpayer, like the one in the 1980 ruling, was growing trees for eventual sale, relief is available even though the taxpayer sells the damaged trees to its usual customers. Under respondent's suggested approach, petitioner would not be entitled to relief because it had choices other than sale; i.e., to further process the damaged trees. Petitioner, under respondent's approach, would be deprived of relief from involuntarily generated gain merely because of happenstance. Under that type of reasoning, petitioner would be denied relief merely because it was a grower of trees and also a manufacturer of products using trees, whereas a similarly situated grower of trees without the ability to use the damaged trees to make products would be entitled to relief, even though its damaged trees might ultimately be manufactured into products by others. The line respondent asks us to draw would be illusive and a matter of conjecture.

Petitioner was growing its trees for harvest when they reached a certain maturity. The damage occurred outside of petitioner's control and forced petitioner to salvage its trees earlier than intended. That situation is indistinguishable from the circumstances set forth in Rev. Rul. 80–175, 1980–2 C.B. 230, where the taxpayer's trees were felled by a hurricane. The fact that the damage was sufficiently partial so as to result in a substantial amount of deferral is not a reason, under the statute, to deny relief.

We read the statute in light of respondent's Rev. Rul. 80–175, supra, which has been outstanding for 22 years.

In view of the foregoing,

Appropriate orders will be issued.

Page 794:

After the first full paragraph, insert:

4. Is Predictability Relevant?

Consider the situation in Willamette Industries, Inc. v. Commissioner, supra, page 97. Although the Tax Court did not consider the predictability of the "casualties" suffered by Willamette—presumably because the Commissioner did not raise the issue—should the predictability of the regularity of the casualties, if that was indeed the case, have been relevant? The Tax Court emphasized that Willamette "was growing its trees for harvest when they reached a certain maturity. The damage occurred outside of [Willamette's] control and forced [it] to salvage its trees earlier than intended." Willamette Industries is a large timber operation. It is virtually certain that every year some percentage of its trees will fall victim to windstorm, fire, and insect damage, and consequently be harvested and processed before their peak maturity. Notwithstanding that Willamette Industries may have intended to harvest all of its trees at maturity, has an "involuntary conversion" really occurred to the extent the harvesting of trees before their optimal maturity was a predictable event? To the extent premature harvesting is predictable and occurs, no one year is any different than any other year; as far as sales revenues and before-tax income are concerned, every year is a normal year. If that is so, why should there be nonrecognition of any portion of the gain on the trees?

CHAPTER 24

TRANSACTIONS INVOLVING LEASED PROPERTY: HAS A SALE OR OTHER DISPOSITION OCCURRED?

Page 825:

At the end of the first full paragraph, insert:

Rev. Proc. 75–21, 1975–1 C.B. 715, has been modified and superseded by Rev. Proc. 2001–28, 2001–1 C.B. 1156. Among the guidelines that the Service will apply to advance ruling requests to determine whether leveraged lease transactions will be treated as leases for tax purposes is the continued requirement that the lessor expects to receive a profit from the transaction apart from the tax benefits arising from the transaction. A significant change is that investments that render the property "limited [to the lessee's] use" for substantially its entire useful life will prevent the transaction from being treated as a lease. Rev. Proc. 2001–29, 2001–19 I.R.B. 1160, sets forth the information and representations required to be furnished by taxpayers in requests for advance rulings on leveraged lease transactions.

CHAPTER 25

CAPITAL GAINS AND LOSSES

SECTION 1. SPECIAL TREATMENT OF CAPITAL GAINS AND LOSSES

Page 830:

Omit the first two paragraphs and insert:

Special rules apply to *capital* gains and losses. A gain or loss that is not capital is referred to as ordinary income or loss. I.R.C. §§ 64 and 65. The importance of the qualification of a gain as a capital gain lies in the preferential tax treatment accorded to gains from the sale or exchange of certain capital assets by individual taxpayers. Generally speaking, gains from the sale of capital assets held for more than one year realized by taxpayers otherwise subject to rates higher than 15 percent are taxed at 15 percent, and taxpayers otherwise subject to rates of 10 or 15 percent are taxed at 5 percent (with a special 0 percent rate capital gains rate for 10 and 15 percent bracket taxpayers in 2008). Some or all of any capital gains realized on the sale of depreciable real estate, however, may be taxed at a maximum rate of 25 percent if realized by a taxpayer otherwise in a tax bracket greater than 15 percent, and gains on the sale of collectibles, e.g., art work, precious gems, gold bullion, antiques, etc., are subject to a maximum rate of 28 percent. If a capital asset is held for one year or less, no preferential rate applies, and the gain, called a "short-term" capital gain, is taxed at the same rate that applies to ordinary income. There is no capital gains preference for corporate taxpayers.

By according capital gains a preference through maximum rates, rather than by a parallel but uniformly proportionally lower rate schedule for each income tax bracket, the benefits of the preferential rates are not proportionate for taxpayers in the different tax brackets—indeed the benefit is random. For example, in the case of gains from capital assets held for more than one year, the benefit of a 5 percent rate to taxpayers who normally are subject to the 10 percent marginal tax bracket is a 50 percent reduction from the rates applicable to ordinary income. For taxpayers who normally are subject to the 15 percent marginal tax bracket, a 5 percent rate for capital gains is a 66⅔ rate reduction from the rates applicable to ordinary income. For taxpayers who normally are subject to the 25 percent marginal tax bracket, a 15 percent rate for capital gains is a 40 rate reduction, while the benefit of a 15 percent rate to taxpayers otherwise subject to the 35 percent marginal tax bracket is approximately a 57 percent reduction from the rates applicable to ordinary income. The rate reduction for taxpayers otherwise in the 28 percent and 33 percent brackets is 46 percent and 54.5 percent, respectively. By according capital gains a preference through maximum rates, rather than by a parallel but uniformly proportionally lower rate schedule for each income tax bracket, the rate reduction generally, but not always, inures disproportionately to taxpayers in the higher tax brackets, who are the taxpayers who realize the vast majority of capital gains.

Page 832:

Replace the tenth sentence of the carryover paragraph with the following:

If C paid the normal maximum rate of 35 percent on his real gain of $700,000, the tax would be $245,000; but the tax on the nominal $800,000 capital gain at a 15 percent rate under § 1(h) is only $120,000.

Pages 834 to 840:

Omit the text of Item "B. CAPITAL GAINS ELIGIBLE FOR PREFERENTIAL RATES" and insert:

1. *General*

The preferential rate in § 1(h) applies only to "net capital gain." The meaning of that term is found in § 1222, which requires a complex netting of long-term and short-term gains and losses. Long-term capital gains and losses are gains and losses recognized with respect to a capital asset held for *more than* one year. All other capital gains and losses are short-term.

Under the pattern of § 1222, long-term gains and losses and short-term gains and losses are separately netted. If the taxpayer has both net long-term capital gain and net short-term capital gain, only the net long-term capital gain meets the statutory definition of "net capital gain" and is eligible for the preference. Net short-term capital gain is taxed at the rates applicable to ordinary income. But if the taxpayer has net long-term capital gain and net short-term capital loss, the net long-term capital gain is reduced by the net short-term capital loss in computing "net capital gain," the amount of capital gain that is accorded the preferential rates.

Once it has been determined that the taxpayer has a "net capital gain" for the year, the elaborate rules of § 1(h) apply different rates to different categories of capital gains. The most preferential rates under § 1(h) are accorded to gains from certain capital assets held more than one year. Gains from such assets are termed "adjusted net capital gains," and are taxed at a rate of 15 percent if the taxpayer is otherwise in the 25 percent or higher marginal tax bracket, and at a 5 percent rate if the taxpayer is otherwise in the 10 or 15 percent marginal tax bracket. "Adjusted net capital gain" does not include: (1) "unrecaptured § 1250 gain," generally speaking, gain on real estate held for more than one year, to the extent of prior depreciation deductions[1] and (2) "28–percent gain." The term "28–percent gain" is defined as the excess of the sum of (a) gains on "collectibles,"[2] and (b) § 1202 gain, over the sum of (c) collectibles losses, (d) net-short term capital loss, and (e) long-term capital loss carryovers to the year in question. I.R.C. § 1(h)(4).

The long-term capital gains excluded from the definition of "adjusted net capital gain" are taxed at a variety of other preferential rates. "Unrecaptured § 1250 gains" are taxed at a maximum rate of 25 percent if the taxpayer's normal marginal rate is 28 percent or higher (and at the taxpayer's normal rate if it is 25 percent or lower). Gains from collectibles held for more than one year are taxed at the taxpayer's normal marginal rate if the taxpayer is subject to a marginal rate of 28 percent or less and at 28 percent if the taxpayer normally is subject to a marginal rate in excess of 28 percent.

The rate structure for § 1202 gains is (believe it not!) even more complex. Section 1202, discussed at page 842 of the text, excludes up to fifty percent of the gain on certain "small business stock." Section 1(h)(7) defines "§ 1202 gain"—the amount excluded from adjusted net capital gains entitled to the 15 percent maximum rate—as the excluded amount, which often, but not always is the same as the included amount. The portion of such gains that are included but which do not exceed the excludable portion of such gains generally are taxed at the taxpayer's normal rates if the taxpayer's marginal rate is 28 percent or lower and at 28 percent under § 1(h)(1)(E) if the taxpayer's marginal rate is 33 percent or 35 percent. The maximum effective tax rate on such gains thus is 14 percent. Any remaining includable gain on the sale of § 1202 stock is taxed at the 15 percent rate, assuming the taxpayer is otherwise subject to the 28 percent or higher rate. See Staff of the Joint Committee on Taxation, General Explanation of Tax Legislation Enacted in 1997, 49, n. 75 (1997).

The basic computation under § 1(h) has five steps. First, under § 1(h)(1)(A), the taxpayer's "normal" statutory rate is applied to the greater of (1) taxable income minus "net capital gain" (i.e., long-term capital gains minus long-term capital losses and net short-term capital losses), or (2) the lesser of (a) the amount of income that ordinarily would be taxed below 28 percent or (b) taxable income minus "adjusted net capital gain."

Assume, for example, four single taxpayers, A, B, C, and D, are all normally subject to the § 1(c) rates (without taking indexing into account) in taxable year 2004. Taxpayer A realized $600,000 of taxable income, of which $100,000 was attributable to salary, $250,000 was attributable to

1. Unrecaptured § 1250 gain is defined in § 1(h)(6) and is discussed at page 947 of the text.

2. Collectibles are defined by § 1(h)(5)(A), through a cross reference to § 408(m), to include works of art, antiques, rugs, gems, metals, stamps, coins, and alcoholic beverages.

gains from the sale of NYSE traded securities held for one year or less (short-term capital gains), $100,000 was attributable to the sale of collectibles held for several years, and $150,000 was attributable to the sale of publicly traded securities held for more than one year (adjusted long-term capital gain). The $100,000 of salary and the $250,000 of short-term capital gains are taxed under the taxpayer's normal rates. Since before taking into account A's capital gains, A is in the 35 percent marginal bracket, the $150,000 long-term gain on the exchange-traded securities and the $100,000 of gain on the collectibles are taxed at preferential rates.

B realized $600,000 of taxable income, of which $200,000 was long-term capital gain from the sale of § 1202 stock (on which B realized a gain of $400,000, only one-half of which was includable in taxable income), and $400,000 was net capital gain from sales of exchange traded securities held for more than one year (adjusted long-term capital gain). Using the $115,000 threshold for the 28 percent bracket in § 1(c) (unindexed for inflation, but as modified by § 1(i)(2)), only $115,000 of taxpayer B's income—a portion of B's § 1202 gain—would be taxed under the normal rate schedules, at 10, 15, 25, and 28 percent; the remaining $85,000 of B's § 1202 gain would be taxed at 28 percent under § 1(h)(1)(E); and all of B's remaining $400,000 of income is taxed at 15 percent.

C realized $600,000 of taxable income, of which $50,000 was attributable to salary, $250,000 was attributable to net long-term capital gains from sales or exchanges of publicly traded securities held for more than one year, and $300,000 was attributable to the sale of an apartment building held for more than one year that had been purchased for $400,000 and sold for $370,000 when its adjusted basis was $170,000. Only C's $50,00 salary income would be taxed as ordinary income—using the 10 percent, 15 percent and 25 percent brackets.

D realized $600,000 of taxable income, of which $10,000 was attributable to net long-term capital gains from sales of collectibles and $590,000 was attributable to net long-term capital gains from sales of publicly traded securities held for more than one year. Only $10,000 of D's income—the $10,000 gain from the sale of collectibles—is taxed at D's normal rates.

The second step in applying the capital gains rate preference mechanism is § 1(h)(1)(B), which provides a maximum rate of 5 percent on the portion of the taxpayer's adjusted net capital gain that does not exceed an amount equal to the threshold for the 25 percent bracket minus the taxpayer's income other than *adjusted* net capital gain (i.e., net short-term capital gain, net long-term capital gain from collectibles, and ordinary income). Only gains recognized with respect to qualified property held for more than one year qualify for this rate. Using the $115,000 threshold for the 25 percent bracket in § 1(c) (unindexed for inflation, but as adjusted by § 1(i)(2)), neither taxpayer A, B, nor C has any income taxed at 5 percent, but taxpayer D has $12,100 of adjusted long-term capital gain that is taxable at the 5 percent rate under this step (the $22,100 threshold for the

25 percent bracket) minus the $10,000 of collectible gains taxed at the normal § 1(c) 15 percent rate (not the § 1(h) preferential 15 percent rate).

The third step in applying the preferential rate rules is the 15 percent rate in § 1(h)(1)(C) applicable to any remaining adjusted net long-term capital gains (or, if less, the taxpayer's taxable income). All of taxpayer A's $150,000 of adjusted net long-term capital gains (from the sales of exchange traded stock held for more than one year) will be taxed at the § 1(h) preferential 15 percent rate. Taxpayer B's remaining $525,000 of taxable income, all of which consisted of adjusted net long-term capital gains (from the sales of exchange traded stock held for more than one year), will be taxed at 15 percent under this provision. Of taxpayer C's remaining taxable income, $350,000—consisting of $250,000 of adjusted net long-term capital gains from the sales of exchange traded stock and $100,000 of gain on the sale of the real estate (the amount by which the $300,00 gain exceeded the $200,000 prior depreciation)—is taxed at 15 percent under this provision. D's remaining $577,900 of adjusted long-term capital gain is taxed at 15 percent under this step.

The fourth step in calculating the tax on capital gains is a 25 percent rate on "unrecaptured section 1250 gain" under § 1(h)(1)(D). Only C has any unrecaptured § 1250 gain, the entire $200,000 gain on the apartment building.

The fifth step, under § 1(h)(1)(E), is to apply a 28 percent rate to any remaining taxable income. Taxpayer A's $100,000 net long-term capital gain on the sale of collectibles would be subject to this step. Taxpayer B's remaining $52,900 of gain on the sale of § 1202 stock also would be taxed at 28 percent. Taxpayers C and D have no income taxable under this provision.

A tabular presentation of the results to A, B, C, and D is as follows:

		A	B	C	D
Salary		$100,000	$ 0	$ 50,000	$ 0
Short-term Capital Gain		250,000	0	0	0
Collectibles Gain		100,000	0	0	10,000
Includable § 1202 Gain		0	200,000	0	0
Unrecaptured § 1250 Gain		0	0	200,000	0
Adj. Long=Term Gain		150,000	400,000	300,000	590,000
Section	*Rate*				
§ 1(h)(1)(A)	10–35%	$350,000	$115,000	$ 50,000	$ 10,000
§ 1(h)(1)(B)	5%	0	0	0	12,100
§ 1(h)(1)(C)	15%	150,000	400,000	350,000	577,900
§ 1(h)(1)(D)	25%	0	0	200,000	0
§ 1(h)(1)(E)	28%	100,000	85,000	0	0

Another layer of complexity was added to the treatment capital gains by the addition of § 1(h)(11) by the 2003 Act. Section 19(h)(11) treats dividends received by the owners of corporate stock as "adjusted net capital gain" under § 1(h)(3), even though the dividend itself (in contrast to the stock) is not a capital asset as defined in § 1221 and dividends are not taken into account in the calculation of "net capital gain" under § 1222. Section 1(h)(11) is discussed at page 116.

2. *Post–2008 Capital Gains Rates*

Prior to the 2003 Act, § 1(h) provided that gains from the sale of capital assets held for more than one year realized by taxpayers otherwise subject to the 15 percent rate bracket were taxed at a 10 percent rate (8 percent if the property had been held for more than five years and was sold after the year 2000), and gains from the sale of capital assets held for more than one year realized by taxpayers otherwise subject to a marginal tax rate of 28 percent or higher were taxed at 20 percent (18 percent if the property had been held for more than five years and was both acquired and sold after the year 2000). As under current law, unrecaptured § 1250 gain on the sale of depreciable real estate could be taxed at a maximum rate of 25 percent, and gains on the sale of collectibles, e.g., art work, precious gems, gold bullion, antiques, etc., could be taxed at 28 percent. The current capital gains rates are scheduled to sunset after December 31, 2008, and if they do, then the pre–2003 version of § 1(h), with its somewhat higher rates, will again be in force. Few tax professionals expect § 1(h) and the sunset date actually to remain unchanged for four years.

3. *Analysis*

If all of the above described rates and changes in rates appear to be hopelessly confusing and completely nonsensical, that is because the rules governing the taxation of capital gains indeed are hopelessly confusing and completely nonsensical. As noted earlier, the capital gains preference has been changed many times. The current rules have no justification in tax policy. They appear to be the arbitrary result of a series of political compromises based on, among other things, using tax expenditures to provide hoped-for economic incentives and targeted tax cuts to taxpayers at particular income levels without directly amending the rate schedules in § 1. Hopefully, this scheme will fall from its own weight and be replaced by a treatment of gains and losses from property transactions that is recognizable as a structural component of an income tax.

4. *Netting of Capital Losses*

If the taxpayer's "net capital gain" for the year consists of gains that are in part offset by losses, it is necessary to determine the order in which losses are subtracted from gains before applying the various rates under § 1(h). Generally speaking, losses are netted first against gains of a like character (by tax rates), with net losses in any grouping being applied to reduce net gains in other rate groupings, moving from the highest rate to the lowest rate, in order, although the statutory mechanics are not particularly straightforward.

Assume, for example, that in 2003 individual E (who is otherwise in the 35 percent bracket) recognized the following long-term capital gains and losses: a $2,500 loss on a collectible, a $2,000 gain on a collectible, a $1,000 gain on the sale of § 1202 stock (with respect to which $1,000 of gain was excluded), a $2,300 gain on exchange traded stock, a $300 loss on exchange traded stock, and a $2,000 gain on the sale of an apartment building, all of which was unrecaptured § 1250 gain. E's net capital gain (as defined in § 1222(11)) is $4,500 (($2,000 + $1,000 + $2,300 + $2,000) – ($2,500 + $300)). The first step in determining E's "adjusted net capital gain," as defined in § 1(h)(3), is to determine the amount of E's 28–percent gain. This amount is $500—the sum of the $2,000 gain on the collectible and the $1,000 gain on the § 1202 stock ($3,000), minus the sum of the $2,500 loss on the collectible—because the collectible gain and loss and the § 1202 gain are both in the "28–percent rate gain" category under § 1(h)(5). Under § 1(h)(3), both the $500 28–percent rate gain and the $2,000 unrecaptured § 1250 gain (totaling $2,500) are then subtracted from the $4,500 net capital gain to leave $2,000 of adjusted net capital gain. This process has effectively netted the $300 long-term capital loss on exchange traded stock against the $2,300 gain on exchange traded stock.

In addition to netting collectible losses against 28–percent rate gains, § 1(h)(4) also applies net short-term capital losses, as defined in § 1222(8), and all capital loss carryovers under § 1212, regardless of the rate category of property that generated the loss in the year it was recognized, against 28–percent gains before netting such losses against gains taxed at a lower rate. If a taxpayer recognizes net losses in the 28–percent rate category, § 1(h)(6) provides for the reduction of unrecaptured § 1250 gain, taxable at 25 percent, by the amount of those losses, thereby applying these losses against gain that otherwise would be taxed at 25 percent before they are applied against losses that otherwise would be taxed at 15 percent. Assume, for example, that in 2003 individual F (who is otherwise in the 35 percent bracket) recognized a $4,000 short-term capital loss on the sale of exchange traded stock, a $5,000 unrecaptured § 1250 gain, and a $6,000 long-term capital gain on the on the sale of exchange traded stock. F's net capital gain is $7,000, consisting of $1,000 of unrecaptured § 1250 gain ($5,000 – $4,000) taxed at 25 percent and $6,000 of adjusted net capital gain taxed at 15 percent. If, however, the short-term capital loss on the sale of exchange traded stock had been $7,000, then F would have recognized a net capital gain of only $4,000, taxed at 15 percent. Under § 1(h)(6), the $7,000 short-term capital loss would completely offset the $5,000 net unrecaptured § 1250 gain. Under § 1(h)(3), which uses net capital gain as a starting point for determining adjusted net capital gain, the remaining

$2,000 of the short-term capital loss effectively would be netted against the $6,000 long-term capital gain on the stock.

If an individual recognizes a net loss with respect to property in the 15–percent rate category and recognizes gains with respect to property in both the 25 percent category (unrecaptured § 1250 gain) and the 28–percent category, the statutory rules result in offsetting the losses against the gains on the 28–percent rate property before offsetting them against the unrecaptured § 1250 gain. Assume that G recognized a $5,000 long-term capital loss on the sale of exchange traded stock, a $10,000 gain on the sale of an apartment building, all of which is unrecaptured § 1250 gain, and a $3,000 long-term capital gain on the sale of a collectible. G's net capital gain (as defined in § 1222(11)) is $8,000 (($10,000 + $3,000) – $5,000). G's 28 percent rate gain (as defined in § 1(h)(4)) is $3,000; G's unrecaptured § 1250 gain under the calculation in § 1(h)(6) is $10,000, but G has only $8,000 of taxable capital gains. This is the maximum amount that can be taxed at 25 percent under § 1(h)(1)(D), and there is no remaining taxable income to be taxed at 28 percent under § 1(h)(1)(E).

Page 841:

Omit the first full paragraph and insert:

No analog of the refined computation used to ascertain net capital gain is necessary in applying the limitation on capital losses in § 1211. Short-term capital losses are subject to the same limitations as long-term capital losses. Section 1212, however, distinguishes between short-term and long-term capital losses in determining which losses are used in the current year and which losses are carried over if the taxpayer has both net short-term and net long-term capital losses. In the case of individuals, the labyrinthine language of § 1212 results in net short-term loss being used before net long-term loss. When capital losses are carried over, in applying the rules of § 1(h) to determine the rate at which gains are taxed in the year to which the losses are carried, the character of the capital assets that generated the carried-over capital loss is irrelevant. All long-term capital loss carryovers, as well as short-term capital loss carryovers in excess of short-term capital gains for the year to which they are carried, are deducted first against long-term capital gains taxed at the 28 percent rate, see I.R.C. § 1(h)(4)(B)(ii) and (iii), then against long-term capital gains taxed at the 25 percent rate (unrecaptured § 1250 gain), see I.R.C. § 1(h)(6)(A), then against gains taxed at the 15 percent rate, and finally against gains taxable at the 5 percent rate. In the case of corporations, all carried-over capital losses are treated as short-term losses in the carryover years.

SECTION 1A. SPECIAL TREATMENT OF CORPORATE DIVIDENDS

INTERNAL REVENUE CODE: SECTION 1(h)(11)(A), (B), (D)(ii).

House of Representatives Report, Jobs and Growth Tax Relief Reconciliation Act of 2003, Conference Report to Accompany H.R. 2

H. Rep. No. 108–126, 108th Cong., 1st Sess. 39–40 (2003).

Under [§ 1(h)(11)], dividends received by an individual shareholder from domestic [and qualified foreign] corporations are taxed at the same rates that apply to net capital gain. This treatment applies for purposes of both the regular tax and the alternative minimum tax. Thus, under the provision, dividends will be taxed at rates of five and 15 percent.[37]

If a shareholder does not hold a share of stock for more than [60] days during the [120]-day period beginning [60] days before the ex-dividend date (as measured under section 246(c)),[38] dividends received on the stock are not eligible for the reduced rates. Also, the reduced rates are not available for dividends to the extent that the taxpayer is obligated to make related payments with respect to positions in substantially similar or related property.

If an individual receives an extraordinary dividend (within the meaning of section 1059(c)) eligible for the reduced rates with respect to any share of stock, any loss on the sale of the stock is treated as a long-term capital loss to the extent of the dividend.

A dividend is treated as investment income for purposes of determining the amount of deductible investment interest only if the taxpayer elects to treat the dividend as not eligible for the reduced rates. [I.R.C. § 1(h)(11)(D)(i)]

Effective date.—The provision is effective for taxable years beginning after December 31, 2002, and beginning before January 1, [2009].

ILLUSTRATIVE MATERIAL

A. DEFINITIONAL ISSUES

Under § 1(h)(11) dividends received by taxpayers other than corporations generally will be taxed at the same rate as long-term capital gains—

37. Payments in lieu of dividends are not eligible for the exclusion. See sections 6042(a) and 6045(d) relating to statements required to be furnished by brokers regarding these payments.

38. In the case of preferred stock, the periods are doubled.

15 percent for taxpayers otherwise taxable at a marginal rate greater than 15 percent (the 25 percent, 28 percent, 31 percent, and 35 percent brackets) and five percent for taxpayers otherwise taxed at a 10 or 15 percent marginal rate (with a special 0 percent rate for 10 and 15 percent bracket taxpayers in 2008). Note that § 1(h)(11) treats dividends as "adjusted net capital gain" under § 1(h)(3), even though the dividend itself (in contrast to the stock) is not a capital asset as defined in § 1221, and dividends are not taken into account in the calculation of "net capital gain" under § 1222. The principal effect of this statutory construction is to extend the 5–percent and 15–percent maximum rates under § 1(h) to dividends received by taxpayers who otherwise are in a higher marginal tax bracket, without permitting capital losses to be deducted against dividend income, except to the extent allowed by §§ 1211 and 1212.

B. ANTI–ABUSE RULES RELATING TO PREFERENTIAL RATES FOR DIVIDENDS

1. *Minimum Holding Period*

The 15 percent preferential rate for dividends, coupled with short-term holding of stock purchased in anticipation of receiving a dividend, creates inappropriate tax arbitrage benefits. Section 1(h)(11)(B)(iii) is aimed at preventing taxpayers from obtaining unwarranted tax benefits n such situations. By incorporating some of the principles of § 246(c), with certain modifications, § 1(h)(11)(B)(iii) provides that the preferential rate for dividends does not apply to any dividends on any share of stock that is held for less than 60 days during the 120 day period beginning on the date that is 60 days before the date on which the stock becomes ex-dividend. (Under stock exchange rules, stock generally becomes ex-dividend three business days before the "record date" for paying dividends.) For preferred stock, if the dividends received are attributable to a period in excess of 366 days, the holding period is extended to 120 days during the 180 day period beginning on the date that is 120 days before the date on which the stock becomes ex-dividend.

Suppose, in the absence of § 1(h)(11)(B)(iii), that during the current tax year individual A realized a $200,000 short-term capital gain on the sale of X Corporation stock and no offsetting capital loss. Absent any other transactions, at a 35 percent marginal tax rate this $200,000 gain would result in a tax of $70,000. Now suppose that shortly before the end of the taxable year, A purchases 100,000 shares of Y Corporation stock for $5,000,000. Before the close of the taxable year, A (1) receives a $200,000 dividend on the Y Corporation stock, and (2) sells the Y Corporation stock for $4,800,000 (the value of the shares having declined as a result of the dividend). A realizes a $200,000 loss on disposition of the Y Corporation shares, because the basis in the stock was not reduced as a result of the dividend. This transaction is uneconomic, because the dividend income is exactly offset by the resulting capital loss. However, at the 15 percent preferential rate, A pays a tax of $30,0000 on the $200,000 dividend received from Y Corporation, while using the $200,000 capital loss on the sale of the Y Corporation stock to offset the $200,000 short-term capital gain on the X Corporation stock that otherwise would have been taxed at the rate of 35 percent, saving $70,000 of tax. Thus, the transaction produces an after-tax benefit of $40,000, even though it produced a break-even before tax cash flow. Under § 1(h)(11)(B)(iii), because the minimum holding period had not been met, the dividend would be taxed at 35 percent—resulting in a $70,000 tax—instead of at 15 percent, and the $40,000 tax arbitrage benefit is eliminated.

2. *Loss recharacterization*

Congress considered § 1(h)(11)(B)(iii) to be adequate to deal with only some of the tax avoidance possibilities created by the availability of the preferential rate for dividends as applied to extraordinarily large dividends. If an extraordinarily large dividend was expected to be paid on stock of a corporation, the investor owning the stock would be willing to hold the stock for the period required to avoid the limitation in § 1(h)(11)(B)(iii). Thus, § 1(h)(11)(D)(i) imposes another limitation when the preferential rate has been claimed with respect to an "extraordinary dividend," as defined in § 1059(c). If an individual receives an extraordinary dividend taxed at the preferential rate, any loss on the sale of the stock on which the dividend was paid is treated as a long-term capital loss to the extent of the dividend, even if the actual holding period of the stock was short-term. As such, under §§ 1222 and 1(h)(4), the long-term capital loss on the sale of the stock with respect to which the dividend was received and the dividend are set-off in determining adjusted capital gain eligible for the 15 percent rate preference.

Consider a variation of the preceding example. Suppose that early in the current tax year individual A realized a $700,000 short-term capital gain on the sale of X Corporation stock and no offsetting capital loss. Absent any other transactions, at a 35 percent marginal tax rate this $700,000 gain would result in a tax of $245,000. Now suppose that soon thereafter, A purchased 100,000 shares of Z Corporation stock for $5,000,000, in anticipation of an extraordinary $700,000 dividend that will be paid later in the year. A holds the Z Corporation stock for more than the holding period required by § 1(h)(11)(B)(iii), and before the close of the taxable year A (1) receives the $700,000 dividend on the Y Corporation stock, and (2) shortly sells the Z Corporation stock, which has not been held for more than one year, for $4,300,000 (the value of the shares having declined as a result of the dividend). A realizes a $700,000 loss on disposition of the Z Corporation shares. Again, the transaction is uneconomic, because the dividend income is exactly offset by the resulting capital loss. However, at the 15 percent preferential rate, A pays a tax of $105,0000 on the $700,000 dividend. Apart from § 1(h)(11)(B)(iii), under § 1222(5), A offsets the $700,000 short-term capital loss on the sale of the Z Corporation stock against the $700,000 short-term capital gain on the X Corporation stock that otherwise would have been taxed at the rate of 35 percent, saving $245,000 of tax. Thus, the transactions involving the Z Corporation stock, which produced a break-even before tax cash flow, effectively reduce the taxes on the sale of the X Corporation stock by $130,000.

Section § 1(h)(11)(B)(iii) deals with this problem by recharacterizing the loss on the Z corporation stock as a long-term capital loss. As a result, under the netting rules of § 1222 and § 1(h), the dividend from Z Corporation, which is treated as § 1(h)(4) net capital under § 1(h)(11), and the deemed long-term capital loss on the Z Corporation stock, which enters into the adjusted net capital gain calculation by virtue of § 1222 and § 1(h)(4) offset each other, leaving the $700,000 gain on the sale of the X Corporation stock to be taxed at 35 percent.

Section 1059(c) defines an extraordinary dividend in terms of the size of the dividend in relation to the shareholder's adjusted basis in its stock, subject to an alternative test that, at the taxpayer's election uses fair market value instead of basis. A dividend is extraordinary if aggregate dividends received in any 85 day period exceed 10 percent of the basis of common stock, or 5 percent of the basis of preferred stock, with respect to which the dividends were paid. Furthermore, if aggregate dividends paid with respect to stock in any one year period exceed 20 percent of the corporate shareholder's basis for the stock, then all such dividends are aggregated and considered to be an extraordinary dividend.

C. ANALYSIS

Reducing the tax rate on dividend income from as high as 35 percent to 15 percent, while wages, interest, and other ordinary income items remain taxable at normal rates, provided an extraordinarily large, highly selective tax cut to a very small number of taxpayers. Taxable dividend income is received by only about 17 percent of all taxpayers and the recipients of dividends tend to be wealthy and at the top of the income pyramid. In 2000, only 11 percent of taxpayers had more than $500 of dividends, and less than 9 percent had more than $1,000. Less than 4 percent of families had dividends over $5,000, but they received 83 percent of all dividends received by individuals. Less than 4 percent of taxpayers whose income was under $20,000 received any dividends, while 58 percent of taxpayers whose income exceeded $200,000 received dividends, and they received much larger amounts of dividend income. The 14 percent of taxpayers whose income exceeded $100,000 collected 72 percent of all dividends, and within that select circle, the 3.8 percent of taxpayers whose incomes exceeded $200,000 collected 47 percent of all dividends. Even those numbers hide the very high concentration of the receipt of dividend income. Within those aggregate numbers, seven tenths of one percent (.7) of all taxpayers—those whose income included more than $25,000 of dividends—collectively received nearly one-half of all dividends. See Leonard E. Burman and David Gunter, 17 Percent of Families Have Stock Dividends, 99 Tax Notes 1261 (May 26, 2003) (statistics are based on most recent data from the Federal Reserve Board's Survey of Consumer Finances).

SECTION 2. DEFINITION OF "CAPITAL ASSET"

Page 845:

After the second full paragraph, insert:

In reading the materials that follow in this chapter note that The Tax Relief Extension Act of 1999 restructured § 1221 to create a subsection (a) in which the categories of property that are not capital assets are listed and a subsection (b) providing certain definitions relating to some of the categories of assets listed in § 1221(a). The 1999 Act also added three additional categories of assets, listed in § 1221(a)(6)–(8), that are excluded from the definition of "capital asset."

A. THE STATUTORY PATTERN

(1) INVESTMENT ASSETS VERSUS ORDINARY BUSINESS ASSETS

Pages 845–871:

In 1999, § 1221(1) was redesignated as § 1221(a)(1).

(2) SECTION 1221(2): REAL PROPERTY AND DEPRECIABLE PROPERTY NOT HELD FOR SALE TO CUSTOMERS

Page 871:

In 1999, § 1221(2) was redesignated as § 1221(a)(2).

(3) SECTION 1221(3): INVESTMENT PROFITS VERSUS REWARDS FOR PERSONAL SERVICES

Page 871:

In 1999, § 1221(3) was redesignated as § 1221(a)(3).

(4) SECTION 1221(4): ACCOUNTS RECEIVABLE

Page 875:

In 1999, § 1221(4) was redesignated as § 1221(a)(4).

Page 875:

At the end of the page insert:

(5) SECTION 1221(a)(6): DEALER–HELD COMMODITIES DERIVATIVE FINANCIAL INSTRUMENTS

Section 1221(a)(6), enacted in 1999, excepts from capital asset classification any "commodities derivative financial instrument" held by a commodities derivatives dealer, unless (1) it is established to the satisfaction of the Commissioner that the particular instrument in question had no connection to the activities of the dealer as a dealer, and (2) the instrument was clearly identified in the dealer's records as having no connection to the dealer activities before the close of the day on which it was acquired, originated, or entered into. The enactment of this section appears to be part of an ongoing effort by Congress and the Treasury to deal with innovative Wall Street financial transactions designed to convert ordinary income into capital gains. Congress was concerned that unless a commodities derivative dealer had elected under § 475 to be treated as a dealer in securities, the character of the gains and losses realized by the commodities derivatives dealer with respect to commodities derivative financial instruments might have been unclear. Congress considered commodities derivative financial instruments to be integrally related to the ordinary course of the trade or business of commodities derivatives dealers, and it concluded that such assets should be treated as ordinary rather than as capital assets. According to the accompanying committee report, however, Congress' concern was not that taxpayers might unjustifiably characterize ordinary income transactions as producing capital gains, but rather that the IRS and courts might impose capital loss limitations on transactions that Congress wanted to accord ordinary loss treatment. See S. Rep. No. 106–120, 106th Cong., 1st Sess. 194–195 (1999).

Section 1221(b)(1) defines a "commodities derivatives dealer" as any person that regularly offers to enter into, assume, offset, assign or terminate positions in commodities derivative financial instruments with customers in the ordinary course of a trade or business. A "commodities derivative financial instrument" is defined in § 1221(b)(2) as any contract or financial instrument with respect to commodities, the value or settlement price of which is calculated by reference to any combination of a fixed rate, price, or amount, or a variable rate, price, or amount, which is based on current, objectively determinable financial or economic information. This definition includes instruments such as swaps, caps, floors, options, futures contracts, forward contracts, and similar financial instruments with respect to commodities, but it does not include shares of stock in a corporation, a beneficial interest in a partnership or trust, a note, bond, debenture, or other evidence of indebtedness, or a contract to which § 1256 applies. See S. Rep. No. 106–120, 106th Cong., 1st Sess. 196 (1999).

(6) SECTION 1221(a)(7): HEDGING TRANSACTIONS

Section 1221(a)(7), enacted in 1999, excepts from capital asset classification any "hedging transaction." This provision, which in effect largely codifies a former version of Treas. Reg. § 1.1221–2 (discussed at page 890 of the text), was intended by Congress to supplant the regulations and any judicially developed doctrines dealing with characterization of hedging transactions. Section 1221(a)(7) facially applies only to a transaction that has been clearly identified as a "hedging transaction" before the close of the day on which it was acquired, originated, or entered into. Section 1221(b)(2)(B), however, requires the Treasury to issue regulations requiring proper characterization of (1) transactions that are in fact hedging transactions but which have not been properly identified and (2) transactions that have been identified by the taxpayer as hedging transactions but which in fact are not hedging transactions. Thus, the identification or non-identification of an asset as a hedging transaction presumably will only create a presumption one way or the other. Because the accompanying committee reports express congressional concern that taxpayers may seek to "whipsaw" the Treasury, the identification rule is highlighted as important. Thus, the recharacterization pursuant to regulations issued under § 1221(b)(2)(B) very well may turn out be a sword only for the Treasury, with the taxpayer's identification (or non-identification) being only a partial shield.

Section 1221(b)(2) codifies the definition of "a hedging transaction" in generally the same manner as the regulations, but broadens the scope by abandoning the "risk reduction" standard of the regulations to one of "risk management" with respect to ordinary property held (or to be held) or certain liabilities incurred (or to be incurred) by the taxpayer. In addition, § 1221(b)(2)(A)(iii) permits the IRS to expand by regulations the definition to include transactions entered into primarily to manage other risks. Congress did not intend that the "risk management" based definition of a hedging transaction extend to "speculative transactions or other transactions not entered into in the normal course of a taxpayer's trade or business." See S. Rep. No. 106–120, 106th Cong., 1st Sess. 195 (1999). The Treasury Department has amended Treas. Reg. § 1.1221–2 to conform to § 1221(a)(7) and that statutory provision's legislative history. See page 123.

(7) SECTION 1221(a)(8): NON–INVENTORY SUPPLIES

Section 1221(a)(8), enacted in 1999, excludes supplies of a type regularly used or consumed by the taxpayer in the ordinary course of a trade or business of the taxpayer. In a number of cases, supplies consumed by the taxpayer or the taxpayer's customer in the course of providing services have been held not to be inventory for purposes of accounting method rules, see, e.g., Osteopathic Medical Oncology and Hematology, P.C. v. Commissioner, 113 T.C. 376 (1999). These cases raise the question of whether such supplies, which have been expensed upon purchase, are capital assets. Section 1221(a)(1) (as former § 1221(1) was renumbered in 1999) does not expressly exclude stocks of previously expensed supplies used in the course of providing services, and neither does § 1221(a)(2). Section 1221(a)(8) eliminates any question in this regard, relegating supplies to ordinary asset characterization. Section 1221(a)(8) also interacts with § 1221(a)(7) to assure that ordinary gain and loss is realized with respect to hedges of prices for supplies, for example, an airline's transactions in jet fuel futures.

B. JUDICIAL LIMITATIONS ON CAPITAL ASSET CLASSIFICATION

(1) THE CORN PRODUCTS DOCTRINE

Page 889:

At the end of the carryover paragraph, insert:

The Court of Appeals for the Federal Circuit affirmed the Court of Claims' decision in *Cenex*. 156 F.3d 1377 (Fed.Cir.1998). The Court of Appeals reasoned that the corporate stock was not "closely related" to the taxpayer's inventory-purchase system because the stock could not fairly be considered an inventory surrogate and the stock transaction did not meet the definition of a hedging transaction. Although stock ownership in the refinery was required to purchase petroleum products, unlike the corn futures which were redeemable for corn by Corn Products Corp., Cenex's stock in the refinery was not redeemable for inventory. Furthermore, unlike the relationship of the values of corn and corn futures, the value of the stock owned by Cenex bore little or no relation to the value of petroleum products inventory items. Thus the loss was not related to the cost of the taxpayer's inventory.

Page 890:

After the second full paragraph, insert:

In 1999 then existing Treas. Reg. § 1.1221–2 and, apparently, the *Corn Products* doctrine more generally, were supplanted by the enactment of § 1221(a)(7), which excepts from capital asset classification any "hedging transaction." This provision largely codified the pre-existing version of Treas. Reg. § 1.1221–2 (discussed at page 890 of the text) and was intended by Congress to supplant the regulations and any judicially developed doctrines, i.e., the *Corn Products* doctrine, dealing with characterization of hedging transactions. See S. Rep. No. 106–120, 106th Cong., 1st Sess. 196 (1999). Treas. Reg. § 1.1221–2 was amended in 2002 to conform to § 1221(a)(7) and that provision's legislative history. Consistent with the legislative history of § 1221, Treas. Reg. § 1.1221–2(a)(3) expressly states that the regulations provide the exclusive means for characterizing gains and losses on hedging transactions as ordinary rather than capital. If a transaction is outside the regulations, gain or loss from the transaction will not be ordinary even if the property is a surrogate for a non-capital asset, the transaction serves as insurance against a business risk, the transaction serves a hedging function, or the transaction serves a similar function or purpose. These regulations appear entirely to supplant the *Corn Products* doctrine, rendering it an historical footnote. Unlike the former version of Treas. Reg. § 1.1221–2, consistent with § 1221(a)(7) and its legislative history, as amended in 2002, Treas. Reg. § 1.1221–2 defines a hedging transaction as one that is entered into to "manage" risk, rather than to "reduce" risk. However, the expressly described hedging transactions—which are stated to be the exclusive list—all focus primarily on risk reduction.

(2) SUBSTITUTE FOR ORDINARY INCOME

Page 897:

After the second full paragraph, insert:

In Davis v. Commissioner, 119 T.C. 1 (2002), the taxpayer won the California lottery and received the right to 20 annual payments of $679,000. Subsequently, he sold a portion of his right to eleven of the fourteen remaining payments for approximately $1,000,000 and reported the gain as long-term capital gain. The Tax Court rejected the taxpayer's argument that the Supreme Court's decision in *Arkansas Best Corp.*, text, page 882, overruled the line of cases that includes Hort v. Commissioner, text, page 891, and Commissioner v. P.G. Lake, Inc., text, page 894, which denied capital gains treatment for the sale of rights to future ordinary income. The court referred to footnote 5 of the *Arkansas Best* opinion, which expressly referred to the continuing vitality of those cases. In holding that the taxpayer realized ordinary income, not capital gain, the Tax Court specifically held that the "right to receive future annual lottery payments does not constitute a capital asset within the meaning of section 1221," without placing much, if any emphasis on the temporal division. Footnote 9 of the *Davis* opinion states:

> It is well established that the purpose for capital-gains treatment is to afford capital-gains treatment only in situations typically involving the realization of appreciation in value accrued over a substantial period of time, and thus to ameliorate the hardship of taxation of the entire gain in one year. * * * [Commissioner v. Gillette Motor Transp., Inc., 364 U.S. 130, 134, 80 S.Ct. 1497 (1960) (citing Burnet v. Harmel, 287 U.S. 103, 106, 53 S.Ct. 74 (1932)).]

Reconsider the *Davis* opinion after reading McAllister v. Commissioner, text, page 897. If the taxpayer in *Davis* had sold all of the remaining lottery payments to which he was entitled, would *McAllister* support capital gain treatment?

SECTION 4. HOLDING PERIOD REQUIREMENT

Page 923:

Omit the last sentence of the carryover paragraph.

Omit the first full paragraph and insert:

Section 1223(11) provides a special holding period rule for property transferred at death that is included in the decedent's gross estate. Under this provision, the person taking from the decedent, such as an executor, administrator, or surviving joint tenant, is deemed to have held the property for more than one year, thereby qualifying gains for the applicable preferential rate under § 1(h) accorded long-term capital gains, even though sale of the property occurs within one year of the date of death of the decedent.

CHAPTER 26

SALE OF ASSETS HELD FOR USE IN A TRADE OR BUSINESS

SECTION 1. QUASI-CAPITAL ASSETS

Page 940:

In the citations to the Code, change "197(f)(8)" **to** "197(f)(7)".

Page 940:

In the citations to the Internal Revenue Code, omit "See also section 1(h)(1)(B), (h)(4)" **and insert** "See also Section 1(h)(1)(D), (h)(4), and (h)(6)."

Omit the third and fourth sentences of the final incomplete paragraph and insert:

Assuming that the taxpayer was an individual in the 35 percent tax bracket and had no other capital gains or losses, the 15 percent maximum rate on adjusted net long-term capital gains in § 1(h) results in a tax liability of $1,500. But if the assets were sold in separate years and the taxpayer had ordinary income against which to claim the loss, the transactions would produce a combined *tax savings* of $6,500. A sale of the first asset in one year would produce a capital gain of $50,000 resulting in a tax liability of $7,500; a sale of the other asset in a separate taxable year would result in an ordinary loss of $40,000, resulting in tax savings of $14,000.

Omit the last sentence of the final paragraph and insert:

Section 1(h)(1)(B) sets the maximum tax rate for capital gain that is "unrecaptured section 1250 gain" at 25 percent, not the more favorable 15 percent rate otherwise available for gains on § 1231 assets held for more than one year.

Page 948:

In the first line of the second paragraph, change "§ 1(h)(1)(B)" **to** "§ 1(h)(1)(D)".

SECTION 2. SALE OF AN ENTIRE BUSINESS

Page 949:

After the Section heading and before the principal case, insert:

INTERNAL REVENUE CODE: Section 1060.

REGULATIONS: Sections 1.1060–1(a), (b)(1)–(7), (c)–(e); 1.338–6(b).

Page 952–953:

Omit the paragraph beginning on page 952 and ending on page 953 and insert:

Section 1060 itself refers to preexisting regulations under § 338(b)(5), which contained a detailed set of rules for allocating the purchase price among the assets sold and purchased. Treas. Reg. § 1.1060–1 (through a cross reference to Treas. Regs. § 1.338–6 and § 1.338–7, which provide the substantive details) requires that the assets of the purchased business be divided into seven classes and the purchase price allocated first among the classes and then among the assets in each class. Class I includes cash and cash equivalents. Class II includes actively traded personal property as defined in § 1092(d), e.g., marketable stock and securities, certificates of deposit, and foreign currency. Class III includes property that the taxpayer must mark-to-market annually for tax purposes and all debt instruments, including accounts receivable, mortgages, and credit card receivables that arise in the ordinary course of business. Class IV includes stock in trade of the taxpayer or other property of a kind that would properly be included in the inventory of taxpayer if on hand at the close of the taxable year, or property held by the taxpayer primarily for sale to customers in the ordinary course of the taxpayer's trade or business. Class V includes all assets not included in Class I, II, III, IV, VI, or VII; this class includes all machinery and equipment, as well as land and buildings (and, if the taxpayer is a corporation, stock of any of its subsidiaries). Class VI includes all § 197 intangibles (as defined in § 197(d)) except goodwill or going concern value. The term "§ 197 intangibles" is intended to be broader than the term "amortizable § 197 intangibles" and includes, for example, § 197 intangibles that are amortizable by the buyer but not by the seller, such as self-created customer lists, employment contracts, supply contracts, etc., as well as business licenses, trademarks and tradenames, and covenants not to compete, even if the covenant is created in the purchase and sale transaction, and patents and copyrights (whether depreciable or amortizable to the seller). Finally, Class VII, which is the residual basis category, includes only goodwill and going concern value. The consideration paid for the business is allocated first to Class I assets based on their fair market value, then seriatim to Class II, Class III, Class IV, Class V, Class VI, and Class VII assets. Within each class, the price is allocated among the assets relative to their fair market values. Since each asset in Classes I–VI generally will be allocated a portion of the price equal to its fair market value, any premium is allocated to Class VII, goodwill and going concern value. Conversely, if a business is purchased for less than its liquidation value, the Class VI (and in some cases, possibly the Class V) assets are allocated an amount less than their individual fair market values. Since almost all § 197 intangibles are amortized over 15 years, the division of § 197 amortizable intangibles between two classes for purposes of determining basis is significant only if some, but not all, of the amortizable intangibles acquired in a single transaction are subsequently sold at a gain, necessitating calculation of individual bases of the intangibles that were sold.

Page 953:

After the first full paragraph, insert:

Notwithstanding the enactment of § 1060, the seller and buyer have a variety of conflicting tax interests in the allocations. From the buyer's side, since all § 197 intangibles are amortized over 15 years, the division of § 197 amortizable intangibles between two classes for purposes of determining basis is significant only if some, but not all, of the amortizable intangibles acquired in a single transaction are subsequently sold at a gain, necessitating calculation of individual bases of the intangibles that were sold. From the seller's side, § 1245 recapture may apply with respect to both Class V assets and Class VI assets, because Class VI contains both amortizable self-created intangibles and purchased intangibles, both of which are subject to § 1245 recapture on sale. But § 1245 applies to Class VI assets only if the goodwill and going concern value were purchased and amortized; self-created goodwill and going concern value, on the other hand, always produce capital gain. Furthermore, the allocation of price between Classes VI and VII on the one hand and between assets within Class V itself can be important. The parties can have differing interests. Class V contains both depreciable and nondepreciable assets, such as land. Purchasers will want to establish as high a fair market value as is possible for depreciable assets and inventory, but for the seller such an allocation may give rise to ordinary income (including § 1245 recapture income) instead of capital gain via § 1231. Generalizations as to which of the seller or purchaser is benefitted by an allocation to Class V versus Class VI are impossible because the analysis is fact specific. Class V contains many assets for which cost recovery under § 168 is more rapid than is cost recovery under § 197 for Class VI and Class VII assets, but it also contains important assets, e.g., buildings and other improvements to real property, for which cost recovery under § 168 is not as rapid as cost recovery for intangibles under § 197.

Page 955:

Replace the citation following the second sentence of the last paragraph with the following:

A covenant not to compete, even if created in the transaction, is a Class VI asset, Treas. Reg. § 1.1060–(1)(b)(7), (d), Ex. 2, while goodwill is assigned to Class VII.

Page 956:

After the second full paragraph, insert:

In Baker v. Commissioner, 118 T.C. 452 (2002), the taxpayer was a State Farm insurance agent, who sold policies exclusively for State Farm as an independent contractor, operating his own agency, developing clients, hiring employees, and paying expenses. Upon retirement, the taxpayer received a "termination payment," returned all of State Farm's property to it, but transferred no identifiable assets of his own. The insurance policies the taxpayer had written were assigned to a successor agent. The Tax Court denied the taxpayer capital gain treatment with respect to the termination payment. He transferred no assets that he owned; the telephone number that the successor agent continued to use and the at-will employment relationships with the office staff were not assets. The taxpayer had no goodwill to transfer, because he transferred nothing to which goodwill could attach. The entire termination payment was ordinary income without regard to the portion of it allocable to a covenant not to compete.

Page 957:

In the fourth and fifth lines of the last paragraph, omit "which has substantially appreciated in value".

CHAPTER 27

TAX SHELTERS

SECTION 2. LIMITATIONS ON TAX SHELTERS

B. PASSIVE ACTIVITY LOSS LIMITATIONS

Page 970:

After the third full paragraph, insert:

St. Charles Investment Co. v. Commissioner, 110 T.C. 46 (1998), rev'd on other issues, 232 F.3d 773 (10th Cir.2000), held that if depreciation deductions are part of a disallowed passive activity loss, the basis of the depreciable asset is nevertheless reduced by the entire otherwise allowable depreciation deduction. On a subsequent sale of the asset, its basis is not recomputed by adding back disallowed depreciation deductions to reduce gain recognized on the sale of the asset. The fact that the depreciation deductions had not produced a tax benefit, and might never produce a benefit unless the conditions for releasing them from suspension under § 469 are met, was irrelevant.

Page 971:

At the end of the carryover paragraph, insert:

To prevent evasion of the passive activity loss limitations by artificially generating passive activity income, Treas. Reg. § 1.469–2(f)(6) recharacterizes as income from a source other than a passive activity any income derived from leasing property to an activity in which the taxpayer materially participates. Thus, in Schwalbach v. Commissioner, 111 T.C. 215 (1998), rental income received by a taxpayer who leased real property to a professional services corporation through which he conducted a dental practice, and in which he owned one-half of the stock, was recharacterized as other than passive activity income, and deductions for the taxpayer's passive activity losses from other sources were disallowed. The same result has been reached in a number of other cases involving similar facts. See Fransen v. United States, 191 F.3d 599 (5th Cir.1999); Sidell v. Commissioner, 225 F.3d 103 (1st Cir.2000); Krukowski v. Commissioner, 279 F.3d 547 (7th Cir.2002).

After the first sentence of the final incomplete paragraph, insert:

Compare Pohoski v. Commissioner, T.C. Memo. 1998–17 (a taxpayer, who resided in California, presented credible evidence that he spent more than 100 hours during the year managing rentals of a Hawaiian condominium unit, which was rented for average rental periods of less than 7 days, and that he spent more time in the activity than employees of a condominium management company, including front desk staff and maid service, but the taxpayer did not present credible evidence with regard to a second Hawaiian condominium unit) with Oberle v. Commissioner, T.C. Memo. 1998–156 (taxpayer who owned a charter yacht did not materially participate in chartering activity by cleaning and winterizing yacht and providing routine maintenance because participation was not more hours than yacht broker, who exercised daily management responsibility of chartering the yacht, including routine cleaning and servicing).

Page 972:
After the second full paragraph, insert:

5. *Self-charged Items*

Section 469(*l*)(2) provides that the Service "shall" promulgate regulations "which provide that certain items of gross income will not be taken into account in determining income or loss from any activity (and the treatment of expenses allocable to such income)." Based on this provision, Prop. Reg. § 1.469–7 (1991) permits offsetting of "self-charged" interest incurred in lending transactions. This rule permits a taxpayer who realizes portfolio interest income from making a loan to a passive activity, usually a partnership in which the lender-taxpayer is a passive partner, to deduct to some extent otherwise disallowed passive activity deductions for interest paid. However, the Service has not issued any regulations dealing with self-charged items other than interest.

In Hillman v. Commissioner, 114 T.C. 103 (2000), rev'd 250 F.3d 228 (4th Cir.2001), the taxpayer performed management services for real estate partnerships in which he was a partner. The taxpayer realized nonpassive income from performing the management services and passthrough passive deductions from the partnerships that paid him for those services. Based on § 469(*l*)(2) and its legislative history, under circumstances analogous to, but not directly covered by, the proposed regulations, the taxpayer offset the passive management fee deductions against the corresponding nonpassive management fee income. The Commissioner argued that the taxpayer could not set off the deductions and income because the Service had not issued any regulations for self-charged items other than interest and that the permitted scope of the offset was thus limited. The Tax Court held, however, that the substantive set-off rule was self-executing and that the taxpayer was entitled to offset the passive management deductions against the nonpassive management income. The court found that such self-charged treatment was congressionally intended not only for interest, but also for other appropriate items, and that there was not any substantial distinction between interest and management fees for this purpose. The Court of Appeals for the Fourth Circuit reversed, finding that "nothing in the plain language of IRC section 469 suggests that an exception to IRC section 469(a)'s general prohibition against a taxpayer's deducting passive activity losses from nonpassive activity gains exists where, as in the present case, the taxpayer essentially paid a management fee to himself." The court reasoned that Hillman's argument for ignoring the plain language of the statute could prevail only if one of "two extremely narrow exceptions to the Plain Meaning Rule" applied: (1) "when literal application of the statutory language at issue produces an outcome that is demonstrably at odds with clearly expressed congressional intent to the contrary" or (2) "when literal application of the statutory language at issue 'results in an outcome that can truly be characterized as absurd, i.e., that is so gross as to shock the general moral or common sense.' " In the court of appeal's view, neither of those situations was present. On remand, 118 T.C. No. 17 (2002), the Tax Court entered judgment for the Commissioner, denying the taxpayer relief from § 469, but in doing so, Judge Gerber stated as follows:

> Unfortunately, petitioners have been snared by the reach of section 469 in, what appears to be, most inequitable circumstances. As we discussed in our prior opinion, section 469 was designed to limit the use of losses generated by passive activities to offset unrelated income generated by nonpassive activities. Although section 469 was designed to stop these practices, Congress recognized that it would be inappropriate to treat certain transactions between related taxpayers as giving rise to passive expense and nonpassive income.
>
> The Secretary was charged with issuing regulations to implement section 469. Commentary contained in the legislative history suggests that self-charged items should be provided for in the regulations. In 1991, regulations were proposed that provided for self-charged interest. Although more than 15 years have passed since the enactment of section 469 and 10 years have passed since the self-charged regulation for interest was proposed, no action has been taken to relieve inequity that may be suffered with respect to self-charged items other than interest.

When Treas. Reg. § 1.469–7 was finalized after the *Hillman* decision was handed down, the Treasury Department declined to expand the proposed regulations to provide relief for taxpayers in Hillman's position, because in 1993 Congress provided relief for real estate professionals in § 469(c)(7). See T.D. 9013, Limitations on Passive Activity Losses and Credits—Treatment of Self–Charged Items of Income and Expense, 67 F.R. 54087 (Aug. 21, 2002).

Page 975:

After the first full paragraph, insert:

DeGuzman v. United States, 147 F.Supp.2d 274 (D.N.J.2001), dealt with the nature of the activities that qualify as a "real estate business" under § 469(c)(7). The taxpayer-wife was a physician with substantial income; the taxpayer-husband reported no taxable income, but performed various services relating to real estate activities, including managing rental real estate owned by the taxpayers and managing the leased premises in which the wife's medical practice was conducted. The taxpayers claimed the losses from rental real estate against the wife's medical income under the § 469(c)(7), based on approximately 800 hours of the husband's "real estate business" activity in the years in question. The court disallowed the deduction. It held that hours providing services relating to property leased from a third party and used in a non-real estate business are not counted toward meeting the 750–hour requirement. Because the husband spent approximately 100 hours in each year managing the wife's medical office facilities, the more-than–750–hour requirement was not met and the rental real estate deductions were disallowed passive activity losses.

After the second full paragraph, insert:

In More v. Commissioner, 115 T.C. 125 (2000), the taxpayer was an individual Lloyds of London underwriter who pledged stock that he owned to secure a letter of credit posted to show that he could cover insurance claims made against him as an underwriter. When he incurred underwriting losses on claims paid, the issuer of the letter of credit sold the stock. Because the stock had been acquired before underwriting activity began, the gain was portfolio income that could not be offset by the passive activity losses from the insurance claims. The court noted however, that if the stock had been purchased with premiums for the insurance business and had been acquired and held for the purpose of "showing means" to cover potential losses, the gain might have been passive.

*

PART VII

TIMING OF INCOME AND DEDUCTIONS

CHAPTER 28

TAX ACCOUNTING METHODS

SECTION 2. THE CASH METHOD

A. INCOME ITEMS

Page 992:

After the third full paragraph, insert:

4. *Cash Option Payoffs of Lottery Annuity Prizes*

Winners of state lotteries and other contests that typically offer an annuity for a term of years as a prize frequently are given the option to take a lump-sum payoff approximating the net present value of the annuity. Ordinarily, the constructive receipt doctrine would require a prize-winner who is given such an option to include currently an amount equal to the lump-sum option even if the taxpayer chose to receive the annuity. On the other hand, if prior to the declaration of a winner, for example, at the time a lottery ticket is purchased, the taxpayer designates in advance whether she will take a lump-sum distribution or an annuity in the event that she wins, the constructive receipt doctrine does not apply. In 1998 Congress apparently concluded that this dichotomy unfairly taxed many lottery winners who opted for the annuity option and it enacted § 451(h), which, if the qualifying conditions are met, ameliorates the application of the constructive receipt doctrine when lottery winners choose to take their winnings in the form of an annuity even if they make the election after the winner of the drawing is announced.

Page 994:

In the third paragraph, Premji v. Commissioner, was affirmed by order, 139 F.3d 912 (10th Cir.1998).

B. DEDUCTION ITEMS

(1) CONSTRUCTIVE PAYMENT AND THE EQUIVALENCE OF CASH—HAS AN ITEM BEEN "PAID"

Page 998:

In the seventh line of the first full paragraph, at the end of the citation to Davison v. Commissioner, insert:

, aff'd per curiam, 141 F.3d 403 (2d Cir.1998).

(2) ADVANCE PAYMENTS—WHEN MUST DEDUCTION OF AN ITEM BE DEFERRED EVEN THOUGH ACTUALLY PAID

Page 1001:

After the carryover paragraph, insert:

B.1. PROPOSED REGULATIONS GOVERNING PREPAYMENTS

Prop. Reg. § 1.263(a)–4(d)(3) (2002) adopts the *Boylston Market Ass'n,* text page 999, principle and specifically requires that prepaid expenses generally be capitalized. However, Prop. Reg. § 1.263(a)–4(f) (2002), adopts the *Zaninovich,* text page 1000, holding and expressly provides that an expenditure to create or enhance intangible rights or benefits that do not extend for more than twelve months after the expenditure is incurred is not required to be capitalized. Amounts paid to create rights or benefits that extend beyond twelve months must be capitalized in full and deducted ratably over the period benefitted.

SECTION 3. THE ACCRUAL METHOD

A. INCOME ITEMS

(1) INCLUSIONS PRIOR TO RECEIPT—THE CONCEPT OF ACCRUAL

Page 1010:

At the end of the second full paragraph, insert:

Section 448(d)(5) was amended in 2002 to limit its application to amounts accrued for the performance of "qualified services" or for other services provided by certain "small businesses." Qualified services include only services in the fields of health, law, engineering, architecture, accounting, actuarial science, performing arts or consulting. Section 448(d)(5) also is available with respect to non-qualified services if the taxpayer's average annual gross receipts (as defined in § 448(c)) do not exceed $5 million.

Page 1013:

After the carryover paragraph, insert:

Rev. Rul. 2003–10, 2003–3 I.R.B. 288, addresses the accrual of income from the sale of goods when an accrual method taxpayer's customer disputes its liability under certain circumstances. The ruling applies the "all events" test of § 451 in three situations: (1) If the taxpayer overbills a customer due to a clerical mistake in an invoice, the customer discovers the error and, in the following taxable year, disputes its liability for the overbilled amount, then the taxpayer accrues gross income in the taxable year of sale for the correct amount. (2) A taxpayer does not accrue gross income in the taxable year of sale if, during the taxable year of sale, the customer disputes its liability to the taxpayer because the taxpayer shipped incorrect goods. (3) A taxpayer accrues gross income in the taxable year of sale if the taxpayer ships excess quantities of goods and in the next year the customer agrees to pay for the excess quantities of goods.

At the end of the second full paragraph, insert:

In Schlumberger Technology Corp. v. United States, 195 F.3d 216 (5th Cir.1999), the taxpayer was not required to accrue a Swiss arbitral award until the period for appeal had expired. Under Swiss law, the arbitral award required judicial confirmation before becoming enforceable and the unappealed award was not judicially confirmed until the period for appeal had lapsed.

(2) ADVANCE RECEIPTS—MAY INCLUSION OF AN ACTUAL RECEIPT BE DEFERRED

Page 1020:

After the carryover paragraph, insert:

In Tampa Bay Devil Rays, Ltd. v. Commissioner, T.C. Memo. 2002–248, the Tampa Bay Devil Rays collected advanced season ticket payments in 1995 and 1996 for the 1998 baseball season, the Devil Rays first season. In the earlier years the Devil Rays were conducting minor league baseball activities—many sports fans think the Devil Rays still are conducting only minor league baseball activities—and deducted the expenses, but did not include the advanced season ticket receipts. Because the receipts would have had to be refunded if the Devil Rays did not play the 1998 season, the court rejected the Commissioner's argument that the receipts for the 1998 season ticket were includable when received in 1995 and 1996 under Schlude v. Commissioner, text, page 1014.

Page 1021:

At the end of the carryover paragraph, insert:

American Express Co. v. United States, 262 F.3d 1376 (Fed.Cir.2001), rejected the Tax Court's holding in *Barnett Banks of Florida, Inc.*, text, page 1020, that the annual fee payments received by a credit card company qualified as "services" under Rev. Proc. 71–21, and held that the Commissioner properly refused to apply the Revenue Procedure.

B. DEDUCTION ITEMS

(1) THE HISTORIC ALL EVENTS TEST

Page 1023:

After the second full paragraph, insert:

The "all events" test requires only that the liability be fixed and owed, not that it actually be payable. For example, in Newhouse Broadcasting Corp. v. Commissioner, T.C. Memo. 2000–244, the taxpayer's book publishing subsidiary business was contractually obligated to pay book authors royalties on all books sold and not returned, even if payment for the books was never received by the publisher. The taxpayer accrued deductions for royalties on all the books it sold during the year. However, the taxpayer did not currently pay to the authors the full amount of the royalties earned on the books that had been sold but set up a "reserve" against returns and held back payment for the portion of the royalties attributable to books expected to be returned. The Tax Court rejected the Commissioner's argument that as a result of this arrangement the all events test had not been satisfied with respect to the amount of royalties equal to the additions to the reserve and not paid. The royalties were legally "owed" to the authors until the books were returned, which was a subsequent event, even if they were not yet payable and might never be payable due to those subsequent events. Thus, the full amount of the royalties was deductible.

Page 1029:

After the fourth full paragraph, insert:

4. *Prepaid Expenses*

Treas. Reg. § 1.461–1(a)(2) operates to prevent the accrual of prepaid expenses, but there has been some controversy regarding the scope of its application. In USFreightways Corp. v. Commissioner, 113 T.C. 329 (1999), rev'd, 270 F.3d 1137 (7th Cir.2001), an accrual method trucking company paid over $4,000,000 to state and local governments for licenses and permits for a one year period that straddled two taxable years. The court held that even if a cash method taxpayer might have been permitted currently to deduct the entire amount of an expenditure that provided a benefit for a period that did not exceed twelve months but which straddled two taxable years—a proposition that it conceded sometimes has been applied but which it did not unqualifiedly endorse in its opinion—an accrual method taxpayer nevertheless must prorate the deduction over the period for which the expenditure provides a benefit. The Seventh Circuit Court of Appeals reversed the Tax Court's decision that § 263 required the deduction to be prorated over the two taxable years, but remanded the case to the Tax Court to consider whether the deduction nevertheless should be prorated over the two taxable years under the "clear reflection of income" standard of § 446(b). Prop. Reg. § 1.263(a)–4(d)(3) (2002) reenforces Treas. Reg. § 1.461–1(a)(2) and requires that prepaid expenses generally be capitalized. However, Prop. Reg. § 1.263(a)–4(f) (2002), adopts the holding of the Court of Appeals in *USFreightways*, supra, and provides that an expenditure to create or enhance intangible rights or benefits that do not extend for more than twelve months after the expenditure is incurred is not required to be capitalized. Amounts paid to create rights or benefits that extend beyond twelve months must be capitalized in full and deducted ratably over the period benefitted.

(2) THE ECONOMIC PERFORMANCE REQUIREMENT

Pages 1042 and 1043:

Omit the second through final sentences of the paragraph beginning on page 1042 and carrying over to page 1043 and insert:

Section 404(a)(11), enacted in 1998, requires that the employee actually receive the compensation income, not merely be required to include it in income, in order for the employer to be entitled to a deduction. The purpose of § 404(a)(11) is to overrule legislatively the result in Schmidt Baking Co. v. Commissioner, 107 T.C. 271 (1996), which allowed a deduction for vacation pay that was not actually paid to the employees but was includable by them within two and one-half months after the close of the employer's taxable year because the obligation was secured by an irrevocable letter of credit purchased by the employer. According to the legislative history, "actual receipt" does not include income inclusion by the employee under the economic benefit doctrine by virtue the employer's obligation being secured by a letter of credit, delivery to the employee of a note (whether or not secured or guaranteed by a third party), or the making of a loan, payment of a refundable deposit, or a contingent payment. Furthermore, "[a]mounts set aside in trust for employees generally are not considered to be actually received by the employee." See H. Rep. No. 599, 105th Cong., 2d Sess., 175 (Conf. Rep. 1998). If the language in the Committee Report is broadly construed, § 404(a)(11) might apply to a transfer to an irrevocable trust for the benefit of an employee, even though in such a case § 83 requires current income recognition by the employee if the employee's rights to the trust corpus and income are not subject to a substantial risk of forfeiture. See pages 994 and 1098 of the text. On the other hand, if the employer actually has paid the funds over to the trust and the employee has included the amount pursuant to § 83, a current deduction is warranted and should be allowed under § 83(h) notwithstanding § 404(a)(11).

SECTION 4. INVENTORY ACCOUNTING

Page 1045:

At the end of the first full paragraph, insert:

RACMP Enterprises, Inc. v. Commissioner, 114 T.C. 211 (2000), held that a construction contracting company that constructed concrete foundations, driveways, and walkways was not required to use the accrual method but could use the cash method to account for its income and expenses for the cost of concrete and other materials. The court held that the taxpayer was in the business of providing services, not of selling merchandise, and that the concrete material was an indispensable and inseparable part of the provision of that service. In Smith v. Commissioner, T.C. Memo 2000–353, the Tax Court found *RACMP Enterprises, Inc.* to be a controlling precedent and held that a flooring contractor who installed custom ordered, and often custom designed, flooring was not required to maintain inventories or use the accrual method. Rather, the taxpayer was a service provider because he installed only floor coverings that were specially ordered from the manufacturer to the customer's specifications and did not maintain a stock of goods to sell to the public (although he did maintain a stock of supplies).

Page 1050:

After the last full paragraph, insert:

E. ELECTIVE SIMPLIFIED TREATMENT FOR SMALL BUSINESSES

In Rev. Proc. 2001–10, 2001–1 C.B. 272, the Service announced that it would permit any business with average annual gross receipts of $1 million or less to use the cash method, rather than the accrual method, and to use a simplified method of accounting for the purchase and sale of inventory items. A business that adopts the cash method under this revenue procedure treats inventory items as materials and supplies that are not incidental under Treas. Reg. § 1.162–3. This treatment requires the taxpayer to capitalize the cost or actual purchases of goods or materials to be resold or incorporated into manufactured products and to offset the capitalized amounts against the amount realized when the goods are resold, but the taxpayer may deduct currently all other manufacturing and handling costs (including labor, warehousing, and other direct and indirect costs that normally must be capitalized under § 263A).

Subsequently, the Service granted certain "small business" taxpayers even greater dispensation from the maintenance of inventories and use of the accrual method of accounting. Citing the Commissioner's discretion under §§ 446 and 471, Rev. Proc. 2002–28, 2002–18 I.R.B. 815, allows qualifying small business taxpayers with "average annual gross receipts" of more than $1 million but less than $10 million to use the cash receipts and disbursements method of accounting, as described in the revenue procedure, with respect to eligible trades or businesses. Any taxpayer whose principal business is the provision of services—including the provision of property incident to those services—is eligible to use the cash method, as are taxpayers whose principal business activity is the fabrication or modification of tangible personal property upon demand in accordance with customer design or specifications. Other businesses qualify unless they are "ineligible." Ineligible businesses include ones that derive the largest percentage of gross receipts from any of the following activities: (a) mining activities within the meaning of North American Industry Classification System (NAICS) codes 211 and 212; (b) manufacturing within the meaning of NAICS codes 31–33; (c) wholesale trade within the meaning of NAICS code 42; (d) retail trade within the meaning of NAICS codes 44–45; and, (e) information industries within the meaning of NAICS codes 5111 and 5122. Lists of the types of businesses within the various NAICS codes for ineligible businesses can be found on the Census Bureau's website. Among the eligible businesses are those that perform services such as janitorial, medical, veterinary, photo developing, and repairs (including auto repair), as well as restaurants, bars, hotels, and funeral homes.

CHAPTER 29

THE ANNUAL ACCOUNTING CONCEPT

SECTION 1. TRANSACTIONAL PROBLEMS

C. INITIAL INCLUSION IN INCOME FOLLOWED BY LATER REPAYMENT

Page 1072:

At the end of the carryover paragraph, insert:

Culley v. United States, 222 F.3d 1331 (Fed.Cir.2000), involved a deduction claimed for restitution paid by a taxpayer who orchestrated a scheme by which his customers, and ultimately the purchaser of his business, were overcharged through his fraud. Pursuant to a criminal conviction, the taxpayer made partial restitution. Although the taxpayer was allowed a § 165 loss deduction, § 1341 did not apply. The court held that § 1341 applies only if at the time of receipt it appeared to the taxpayer that he had an unrestricted right to the funds subsequently repaid. Thus, a deduction for restitution of funds obtained by fraud is not subject to § 1341, even though it may have appeared to the defrauded parties at the time that they paid him that the taxpayer had an unrestricted right to the funds.

After the carryover paragraph, insert:

Conversely, § 1341 is not necessarily applicable merely because a deduction is allowed for a payment of a disputed amount. In Chernin v. United States, 149 F.3d 805 (8th Cir.1998), the taxpayer was involved in litigation with his former employer regarding the employer's claim that the taxpayer had embezzled funds by authorizing bonuses to be paid to himself. The taxpayer had reported the bonuses as income. While the litigation was pending, the taxpayer's bank account was garnished and the taxpayer claimed a deduction for that year under § 461(f), which was allowed. He was not permitted, however, to compute the deduction under § 1341. The court held that the § 1341(a)(2) requirement—that it be established that the taxpayer does not have an unrestricted right to the income—requires that the amount actually be repaid to the original payor. The fact that a deduction is allowed under § 461(f) because funds to pay a deductible expense have been put in escrow beyond the taxpayer's control is not sufficient to invoke § 1341 relief.

SECTION 4. NET OPERATING LOSS CARRYOVER AND CARRYBACK

Page 1079:

At the end of the first full paragraph, insert:

The 2002 Act added § 172(b)(1)(H) to extend the general NOL carryback period from two years to five years for NOLs arising in taxable years ending in 2001 and 2002. Section 172(j) allows the taxpayer to make an irrevocable election to waive the special five-year carryback period; if a taxpayer elects to waive the five-year carryback period, the NOLs are subject to the normal rules.

Page 1084:

At the end of the last paragraph, insert:

The 1998 Act made § 1301 a permanent provision.

CHAPTER 30

DEFERRED COMPENSATION ARRANGEMENTS

SECTION 2. TRANSFERS OF PROPERTY FOR SERVICES

B. SECTION 83

Page 1110:

After the first sentence of the second full paragraph, insert:

Venture Funding Ltd. v. Commissioner, 110 T.C. 236 (1998), aff'd by order, 198 F.3d 248 (6th Cir.1999), upheld the validity of Treas. Reg. § 1.83–6(a). The Regulation provides that an employer's deduction is the amount actually included by the employee on the employee's return, not the amount properly includable. The Regulation also provides, however, that an amount is deemed to have been "included" by the employee if the employer files with the Service a timely information return (e.g., a Form W–2 or 1099–MISC) reporting the payment to the employee. But if the employer fails to file an information return and the employee fails to include the amount in income, the employer is not entitled to a deduction.

SECTION 3. QUALIFIED PENSION PLANS

Page 1121:

After the fist paragraph of the *ILLUSTRATIVE MATERIAL*, insert:

The 2001 Act made extensive technical changes in the rules governing qualified pension plans. The unindexed benefits limit for defined contribution plans has been increased from $90,000 to $160,000. The unindexed contributions limit for defined benefit plans has been increased from $30,000 to $40,000. Special rules in new § 414(v) allow increased elective contributions to defined contribution plans by employees age 50 or older. The amendments to the qualified pension plan rules permit extensive rollovers between qualified plans and between qualified plans and IRAs as employees change jobs.

CHAPTER 31

DEFERRED PAYMENT SALES

Page 1130:

After the second full paragraph, insert:

(d) *Deferred Section 1031 Like-kind Exchanges*

If a properly structured deferred § 1031 like-kind exchange, see text, page 790, ultimately fails to qualify for nonrecognition under § 1031 because the taxpayer receives cash instead of like-kind property, installment reporting under § 453 may be available. See Treas. Reg. § 1.1031(k)–1(j)(2). Smalley v. Commissioner, 116 T.C. 450 (2001), involved an interesting application of this rule. In 1994, the taxpayer entered into a deferred exchange agreement under which, through a qualified intermediary, he relinquished timber-cutting rights on land he owned in fee; the ultimate purchaser paid cash to a qualified escrow account as defined in Treas. Reg. § 1.1031(k)–1(g)(3). In 1995, within the period required by § 1031(a)(3), the taxpayer received fee simple interests in three parcels of real estate. The Commissioner asserted that the taxpayer recognized gain in 1994 because the timber cutting rights were personalty and thus not like kind to a fee simple in timber land. The Tax Court held that regardless of whether the timber cutting rights surrendered and the fee land received were like kind, no income was realized in 1994. At the beginning of the exchange period, the taxpayer had a bona fide intent to enter into a deferred exchange of like-kind property within the meaning of Treas. Reg. § 1.1031(k)–1(j)(2)(iv), and under Treas. Reg. § 1.1031(k)–1(g)(3) he was not in either actual or constructive receipt of property in 1994. If the transaction was not a like kind exchange, it was a § 453 installment sale. Whether the transaction was a like-kind exchange, or an installment sale with payment received in 1995, is a question that affects the basis of the property received, but that question was not before the court.

Page 1134:

After the third full paragraph, insert:

3. *Contracts for Deed Sales Transactions*

In Keith v. Commissioner, 115 T.C. 605 (2000), the taxpayer sold residential real property through contracts for deed, under which the buyers obtained possession, assumed responsibility for taxes, insurance, and maintenance, and agreed to make monthly payments, with interest, of the purchase price. Under the sales contracts, a warranty deed would be delivered to a buyer only upon full payment; any default by a buyer voided the contract. In that event, the taxpayer could retain, as liquidated damages, all amounts previously received, but the buyer was not liable for the remaining unpaid balance. The taxpayer, who reported on the accrual method, did not report any gain attributable to the contracts until the year in which full payment had been received and title was transferred. The Tax Court held that because under state law the benefits and burdens of ownership had passed to the buyers upon execution of the contract and transfer of possession, notwithstanding the "nonrecourse" nature of the buyers' obligations, the sales were completed in the year the contracts were executed. Because the sales were dealer dispositions to which § 453 did not apply, the gain from the dispositions had to be recognized in that year.

Page 1135:

After the second full paragraph, insert:

The Tax Relief Extension Act of 1999 amended § 453A(d) to apply the "pledge as recognition" rule whenever a taxpayer holding an installment obligation has the right to satisfy all or any portion of his own debt to any creditor by transferring the installment obligation.

PART VIII

THE TAXABLE UNIT

CHAPTER 33

TAXATION OF FAMILY

SECTION 1. THE CHOICE OF TAXABLE UNIT

B. HISTORICAL BACKGROUND

Page 1161:

At the end of the first full paragraph, insert:

The 2001 Act substantially revised the calculation of the phase-out of the earned income credit to reduce the marriage penalty inherent in the phase-out rules.

After the second full paragraph, insert:

In the 2001 Act, Congress half-heartedly responded to demands for relief from the "marriage penalty" with two changes. First, the 2001 Act increased the basic standard deduction under § 63, text, page 653, for married couples filing a joint return to twice the basic standard deduction for unmarried individuals filing a single return. Second, the 2001 Act increased the width of the 15 percent rate bracket for married couples filing jointly relative to unmarried individuals filing a single return. The upper limit of the 15 percent bracket for married couples filing a joint return will be double upper limit of the 15 percent bracket for unmarried individuals filing a single return. The effective date of both of these changes is delayed to 2005, and even then they are phased in over five years, with the result that the full effect of the changes will not be in force until 2009. Like all of the other amendments to the Code in the 2001 Act, however, these changes sunset on December 31, 2010.

SECTION 3. TAX ASPECTS OF DIVORCE AND SEPARATION

A. ALIMONY AND CHILD SUPPORT

Page 1172:

After the citation following the third sentence of the first full paragraph, insert:

Such a designation does not need to mimic the statutory language of § 71(b)(1)(B); a statement in the divorce instrument that a series of cash payments is intended to be a property settlement payable in installments subject to § 1041 will remove the payments from the alimony regime. Estate of Goldman v. Commissioner, 112 T.C. 317 (1999), aff'd by order sub. nom. Schutter v. Commissioner, 242 F.3d 390 (10th Cir.2000), involved the treatment of payments of $20,000 per month for 240 months, subject to termination on the payee's death. According to the divorce instrument the payments were "in furtherance of the equitable division of property." The court held that the payments were not alimony because the divorce instrument provided that all payments thereunder were subject to § 1041 and would be "reported . . . in such a manner as no gain or loss shall be recognized," consistent with the "intent of reporting the division and transfers of property as a non-taxable event."

After the third full paragraph, insert:

The requirement that payments terminate upon death can affect the characterization of payments that seem far removed from being a disguised property settlement. Many states provide for temporary unallocated "family support" payments from one spouse to the other during the time the divorce action is pending. An unallocated family support allowance that under either the terms of the agreement or state law does not terminate upon the payee's death cannot qualify as alimony by reason of § 71(b)(1)(D). In Lovejoy v. Commissioner, 293 F.3d 1208 (10th Cir.2002), neither the divorce instrument nor state law provided that a temporary unallocated family support allowance *pendente lite* terminated upon wife's death. Even though her death would have abated the divorce, state law provided that child support orders were not terminated by the custodial spouse's death. The payments were not deductible by the husband and not includable by the wife.

Page 1174:

In the eighth line of the carryover paragraph, at the end of the citation to Ribera v. Commissioner, insert:

, aff'd by order, 139 F.3d 907 (9th Cir.1998).

At the end of the carryover, insert:

In Burkes v. Commissioner, T.C. Memo. 1998–61, the husband's payment of the wife's attorney's fees as "additional alimony" was taxable to her under § 71. Under the applicable state law, a "support alimony" obligation terminated on the payee's death but a "property settlement" alimony obligation did not so terminate. An examination of the language of the divorce instrument as a whole indicated that the husband's obligation to pay the wife's attorney's fees was "support alimony" under state law.

Page 1175:

After the first full paragraph, insert:

In Hammond v. Commissioner, T.C. Memo. 1998–53, a husband was obligated to make separate and distinct payments of "child support" in the amount of $1,140 per month until the couple's child attained the age of 18, died, married, or joined the military, and "alimony" of $2,012 per month until the earlier of the child's eighteenth birthday or the wife's remarriage. Because the $2,012 per month alimony payments terminated immediately after the child's eighteenth birthday, those payments were classified as child support, not alimony, for purposes of § 71.

B. PROPERTY SETTLEMENTS

Page 1181:

After the second full paragraph, insert:

In Young v. Commissioner, 240 F.3d 369 (4th Cir.2001), a former husband defaulted on a $1.5 million promissory note that he had given his former wife in a divorce settlement in 1989. She sued him on the note, and in 1992 he satisfied the judgment in the suit by transferring to her a parcel of real estate that he had received in the divorce. She subsequently sold the property. The court held that the husband's transfer of the real estate to the wife was "incident to the divorce." Accordingly, under § 1041, the husband recognized no gain on the transfer and the wife held it with a transferred basis from her former husband, which resulted in her realizing a significant gain on the sale. The court rejected the wife's argument that she had received the property as a "judgment creditor," finding that the only relevant status was her status as a "former spouse." According to the court, the sole reason for the 1992 transfer of the real estate was to resolve ongoing disputes that originated in the divorce.

In Yankwich v. Commissioner, T.C. Memo. 2002–37, the taxpayer's former husband was required by the divorce instrument to remit to her, as he received payments on a promissory note owned by him, amounts equal to the interest and principal received. There was no transfer of actual beneficial ownership of the note itself, and thus § 453B(g) did not apply to treat the note as transferred to the wife in a § 1041 transaction. Nevertheless, the court treated the husband as having transferred to the wife a note with a principal amount, interest rate, and payment schedule identical to the underlying note. Thus, amounts received representing principal were excludable under § 1041, but amounts received representing interest were not excludable.

Page 1183:

After the second full paragraph, insert:

After initially taking the position in Rev. Rul. 87–112, 1987–2 C.B. 207, text, page 1182, that § 1041 does not apply to a mere right to collect accrued but unpaid income, the Service has reversed course and has ruled that § 1041 applies to vested rights to receive income already earned. In Rev. Rul. 2002–22, 2002–19 I.R.B. 849, the Service held that § 1041 applies to a transfer, pursuant to a divorce, of interests in nonstatutory stock options and nonqualified deferred compensation benefits. The former spouse to whom the rights are transferred, and not the transferor-employee spouse, must recognize income upon exercise of the stock options or receipt of the deferred compensation. More generally, the ruling states that the Service will not apply assignment of income principles to override § 1041 except in cases in which the rights to the transferred income are not vested at the time of the transfer. Rev. Rul. 2002–22 indicates that the Service will continue to apply Kochansky v. Commissioner, text page 1183, in the latter instance.

Page 1185:

After the first full paragraph, insert:

In Read v. Commissioner, 114 T.C. 14 (2000), aff'd sub. nom. Mulberry Motor Parts, Inc. v. Commissioner, 273 F.3d 1120 (11th Cir.2001) (per curiam), the Tax Court applied a different test than it had previously applied when dealing with redemptions in connection with divorces to which § 1041 might be applicable through Temp. Reg. § 1.1041–1T(c), Q & A–9. Mr. and Mrs. Read owned substantially all of the stock of Mulberry Motor Parts, Inc. (MMP). When they divorced, the final judgment ordered (1) that Mrs. Read sell to Mr. Read, or at Mr. Read's election to MMP or MMP's ESOP plan, all of her MMP stock, and (2) that Mr. Read, or at Mr. Read's election MMP or MMP's ESOP plan, pay $838,724 to Mrs. Read ($200,000 down and the balance by interest bearing note). Mr. Read elected to cause MMP to purchase and pay for Mrs. Read's stock, and the transaction was so structured. Mrs. Read argued that she was entitled to nonrecognition under § 1041(a) and Temp. Reg. § 1.1041–1T(c), Q & A–9, which treats certain transfers to third parties as a transfer of property by the transferring spouse directly to the nontransferring spouse that qualifies for nonrecognition treatment under § 1041 followed by an immediate transfer of the property by the nontransferring spouse to the third party in a transaction that is not subject to § 1041. As a corollary, Mr. Read would have a redemption treated as a dividend under the standards of § 302. Mr. Read argued that § 1041(a) and Temp. Reg. § 1.1041–1T(c), Q & A–9, were inapplicable because he never had an unconditional obligation to purchase Mrs. Read's MMP stock. Under this view, Mr. Read recognized no income, and Mrs. Read recognized gain on the redemption of her stock under § 302(b)(3). The Commissioner took the position that he was a mere stakeholder (a claim that, by the way, was not true; more taxes would be collected if Mrs. Read's position prevailed than if Mr. Read's position prevailed) and had issued deficiency notices to both taxpayers in the joined cases to avoid a whipsaw, but the Commissioner argued that Mrs. Read "has the better argument." In a reviewed opinion, with eight judges in the majority and seven dissenting, the Tax Court agreed with the Commissioner and Mrs. Read. The court held that in cases involving corporate redemptions in a divorce setting, the normal tests for determining whether the redemption occurred on behalf of the continuing shareholder, i.e., that the continuing shareholder was relieved of a primary and unconditional obligation to purchase the stock, is not the appropriate standard to apply to determine whether the transfer of property by the transferring spouse to a third party is on behalf of the nontransferring spouse within the meaning of Temp. Reg. § 1.1041–1T(c), Q & A–9. Applying the common, ordinary meaning of the phrase "on behalf of" in Q & A–9, Mrs. Read's transfer of her stock to MMP was a transfer of property by Mrs. Read to a third party on behalf of Mr. Read within the meaning of the regulation. Thus, under § 1041(a), no gain was recognized by Mrs. Read and Mr. Read recognized a dividend. The majority reasoned that Hayes v. Commissioner, text page 1185, did not limit the treatment of a redemption of one divorcing spouse's stock as a § 1041 transfer by that spouse and a dividend to the nonredeeming spouse. It distinguished Blatt v. Commissioner, text, page 1185, because in that case the record did not establish that the corporation acted on behalf of the husband in redeeming the wife's stock; and the majority attempted to distinguish the Tax Court's prior opinion in Arnes v. Commissioner, text, page 1184, as involving an instance in which the husband did not have an unconditional obligation to acquire the wife's stock. Several dissenting opinions all argued, in one way or another, that the primary-and-unconditional-obligation standard that generally applies to determine whether a redemption of corporate stock outside the divorce context was on behalf of a continuing shareholder was the appropriate standard to apply, that nothing in Temp. Reg. § 1.1041–1T(c), Q & A–9, indicated otherwise, and that on the facts Mr. Read did not have a primary and unconditional obligation to purchase Mrs. Read's stock. Another dissent argued that Temp. Reg. § 1.1041–1T(c), Q & A–9, never should apply to redemptions like those in any of these cases. Craven v. United States, 215 F.3d 1201 (11th Cir.2000), followed *Read*.

In early 2003, the Treasury Department attempted to clarify this confused line of cases by issuing regulations specifically dealing with redemptions of stock of one of the spouses in connection with a divorce when the other spouse continues to own stock of the corporation. Treas. Reg. § 1.1041–2. Under Treas. Reg. § 1.1041–2(a)(1), the determination of whether there is a constructive dividend under "applicable tax law," meaning the unconditional obligation test of Wall v. United States, 164 F.2d 462 (4th Cir.1947) and Sullivan v. United States, 363 F.2d 724 (8th Cir.1966) (see text page 865), notwithstanding Temp. Reg. § 1.0141–1T(c), Q&A 9. If the redemption of stock from one spouse (the transferor spouse) is treated as a constructive dividend to the other spouse (the nontransferor spouse) under applicable tax law, then the transferor spouse will be treated as transferring the stock to the other, nontransferor, spouse in exchange for the redemption proceeds in a nonrecognition exchange under § 1041. The transferor spouse does not recognize gain or loss. The nontransferor spouse is not treated as receiving a constructive distribution subject to § 302, which generally results in a dividend under § 301, and then transferring the distributed money or property to the transferor spouse. Prop. Reg. § 1.1041–2(a)(2) and (b)(2). If the redemption is not treated as a constructive dividend to the nontransferor spouse under existing law, e.g. the nontransferor spouse is not subject to an unconditional obligation with respect to the redemption, then the transaction will be taxed in accordance with its form; the transferor spouse will be treated as receiving a taxable distribution under § 302. Treas. Reg. § 1.1041–2(a)(1) and (b)(1). The preamble to the proposed regulations states that "if the rules of the proposed regulations had applied in the *Arnes* case, because the husband did not have a primary and unconditional obligation to purchase the wife's stock, the redemption would have been taxed in accordance with its form with the result that the wife would have incurred the tax consequences of the redemption." REG–107151–00, 66 F.R. 40659 (Aug. 3, 2001).

The following example illustrates the application of Treas. Reg. § 1.1041–2 in a typical case. Assume that H and W each own 50 percent of the stock of X Corporation. H's basis for his stock is $10,000; W's basis for her stock is $12,000. Neither H nor W has any pre-existing unconditional obligation to purchase the other's stock of X Corporation. The divorce instrument requires W to sell her stock to X Corporation for $50,000 and she does so. Under Treas. Reg. § 1.1041–2, W recognizes a capital gain of $38,000 ($50,000 − $12,000), and H has no tax consequences. On the other hand, if the divorce instrument required H to purchase W's stock for $50,000 and H caused X Corporation to repurchase her stock instead of purchasing it personally, W is treated as transferring her X Corporation stock to H for $50,000 and pursuant to § 1041 she does not recognizes her gain. H takes a $12,000 basis in the stock received from W, which he is treated as selling back to the corporation. Because H owned 100 percent of the stock of X Corporation both immediately before and after the repurchase, under §§ 301 and 302 he generally is treated as receiving a dividend of $50,000, all of which is included in gross income, with out any basis offset, albeit at a preferential rate (see page 116).

Special rules permit the spouses to agree to treat the redemption inconsistently with the generally applicable tax law regarding constructive dividend treatment. Treas. Reg. § 1.1041–2(c)(1) provides that even though the redemption results in a constructive dividend distribution to the nontransferor spouse under applicable law, if the spouses agree in the divorce or separation instrument (or other valid written agreement) that the redemption will be treated as a redemption distribution to the transferor spouse, then the redemption will be treated as a redemption taxable to the transferor spouse notwithstanding that the redemption otherwise would result in a constructive dividend distribution to the nontransferor spouse. Under this rule, in the second variation of the original example—where H had a personal obligation to purchase W's stock, H and W nevertheless could amend the divorce instrument to agree that rather than H recognizing a $50,000 dividend and W having no tax consequences, W would recognize a $38,000 gain and H would have no tax consequences.

Conversely, Treas. Reg. § 1.1041–2(c)(2) provides that even though the redemption does not result in a constructive dividend distribution to the nontransferor spouse under applicable law, if the spouses agree in the divorce or separation instrument (or other valid written agreement) that the redemption will be treated as a redemption distribution to the transferor spouse, then the redemption will be treated as a transfer by the transferor spouse of the redeemed stock to the nontransferor spouse in exchange for the redemption proceeds, and the receipt of the redemption proceeds by the nontransferor spouse from the corporation. Thus, the spouses can agree to nonrecognition treatment for the transferor spouse who is redeemed, coupled with constructive dividend treatment for the other. Thus, in the first variation of the above example—where H had no personal obligation to purchase W's stock, H and W nevertheless could agree that rather than W recognizing a $38,000 gain and H having no tax consequences, H would recognize a $50,000 dividend and W would have no tax consequences.

CHAPTER 34

SHIFTING INCOME AMONG TAXABLE UNITS

SECTION 2. INCOME FROM PROPERTY

Page 1215:

After the carryover paragraph, insert:

The 2001 Act extensively revised § 529. The most significant change is the amendment of § 529(c)(3)(B) to provide a complete exclusion for in-kind benefits, e.g., tuition waivers, and distributions expended for qualified higher education benefits. Section 529 qualified tuition plans thus have been transformed from vehicles to secure an effective assignment of investment income to a lower bracket taxpayer to a vehicles to provide tax exempt income. In addition, § 529(b)(1) has been amended to permit private institutions of higher education to establish trusts that can qualify for § 529 treatment. Such private § 529 plans can qualify, however, only with respect to purchases of tuition credits or certificates on behalf of the designated beneficiary; cash contribution to a savings plan are not permitted with respect to private § 529 qualified tuition programs. Section 529(c)(3)(C) rollover treatment has been extended to transfers from one plan to another plan on behalf of the same beneficiary. This new rule will facilitate transfers from state qualified tuition plans to new private qualified tuition plans. If a beneficiary receives distributions from both a § 529 qualified tuition plan and from an EIRA, see text, page 342, in the same year and the combined distributions exceed the qualified expenditures, new § 529(c)(3)(B)(vi) requires that qualifying expenses be allocated among distributions from the § 529 plan and the EIRA to determine how much of the distribution form each is excludable. Finally, even though a taxpayer—usually the student's parent—may claim the HOPE credit or Lifetime learning credit under § 25A, text, page 730, with respect to a student, the exclusion under § 529(c)(3) is available—to the student—for distributions from a § 529 plan with respect to the student as long as the distributions from the § 529 plan are not traced to the expenditures with respect to which the credit is claimed. I.R.C. § 529(d)(2)(C)(i). In other words, both benefits are available as long as qualified expenditures for the year equal or exceed the sum of the distributions form the § 529 plan and the base on which the § 25A credit is calculated. Like all of the other amendments to the Code in the 2001 Act, however, these changes sunset on December 31, 2010.

PART IX

ALTERNATIVE MINIMUM TAX

CHAPTER 36

ALTERNATIVE MINIMUM TAX

Page 1272:

After the fourth sentence of the first full paragraph, insert:

See Holly v. Commissioner, T.C. Memo. 1998–55 (alternative minimum tax applied to taxpayer with adjusted gross income of under $50,000 because he had $33,000 of miscellaneous itemized business deductions, mostly unreimbursed employee business expenses).

After the second full paragraph, insert:

The 2001 and 2003 Acts combined to increase the alternative minimum tax exemption amount for 2001 and 2002 to $35,750 for single taxpayers and $49,000 for married taxpayers filing joint returns, and for 2003 and 2004 to $40,250 for unmarried taxpayers and to $58,000 for married taxpayers filing joint returns. Because the regular tax personal and dependency deductions are added back in computing alternative minimum taxable income and the lump sum alternative minimum tax exemption does not reflect the number of the taxpayer's dependents, a taxpayer with none of the preference items listed in § 57 and few, if any, of the § 56 adjustments, may be subject to the alternative minimum tax. Indeed, alternative minimum tax liability can result solely from the combination of a large number of children claimed as dependents, and relatively modest amounts of itemized deductions that have been disallowed in computing the alternative minimum tax. See Klaassen v. Commissioner, T.C. Memo. 1998–241, aff'd by order, 182 F.3d 932 (10th Cir.1999) (married taxpayer filing jointly with $83,056 of gross income, $10,996 of medical expenses, $3,264 of state and local taxes, and 12 personal exemptions had a $1,085 AMT liability). This result has prompted many members of Congress to call for reform of the alternative minimum tax.

After the third full paragraph, insert:

(A special rule in § 56(d)(1)(A), as amended in 2002, allows AMT NOL carrybacks arising in 2001 and 2002, and AMT NOL carryforwards to 2001 and 2002, to offset 100 percent of AMTI.)

Page 1273:

Delete the second paragraph and insert:

As Congress creates new incentive tax preferences, it must determine whether to subject such preferences to the alternative minimum tax. The 1993 Act created a preferential exclusion under § 1202 for gains realized on the sale of stock in certain "small business" corporations held for more than five years. Consequently, a new tax preference item was added to the minimum tax computation by § 57(a)(7). As originally enacted, when the preferential rate for long-term capital gains was 20 percent, § 57(a)(7) required that forty-two percent of the amount excluded under § 1202 be added back in computing alternative minimum taxable income. When the preferential rates for long-term capital gains were reduced to 15 and 5 percent in the 2003 Act, § 57(a)(7) was amended to require that only seven percent of the amount excluded under § 1202 be added back in computing alternative minimum taxable income. Unlike most preferences, which are totally denied in the alternative minimum tax system, this preference is partially allowed. Under the original version of § 57(a)(7), as a result of adding back 42 percent of the excluded amount, if the taxable gain were taxed at the 28 percent maximum alternative minimum tax rate, the effective tax rate on the entire gain was approximately 20 percent, the rate that then generally applied for regular tax purposes to long-term capital gains. Under the current version of § 57(a)(7), as a result of adding back 7 percent of the excluded amount, if the taxable gain is taxed at the 28 percent maximum alternative minimum tax rate, the effective tax rate on the entire gain is approximately 15 percent, the maximum rate that generally applies for regular tax purposes to long-term capital gains.

Delete the third full paragraph and insert:

In light of the historic purpose of the alternative minimum tax, the 1997 Act added an anomalous feature—an alternative minimum tax preferential rate for long-term capital gains. I.R.C. § 55(b)(3). To the extent that capital gains are attributable to prior depreciation deductions on real estate, the maximum rate is 25 percent, as under the regular tax. The maximum rate on all other net long-term capital gains is bifurcated. Prior to May 6, 2003, net long-term capital gains up to an amount equal to the threshold for the 28 percent bracket for ordinary income under the regular tax for the taxpayer's filing status were subject to an alternative minimum tax rate of 10 percent; any remaining long-term capital gains were taxed at 20 percent. Because the 2003 Act reduced the rate on long-term capital gains under § 1(h) after May 6, 2003, net long-term capital gains up to an amount equal to the threshold for the 25 percent bracket for ordinary income under the regular tax for the taxpayer's filing status are subject to an alternative minimum tax rate of 5 percent; any remaining long-term capital gains are taxed at 15 percent. Unlike the regular tax, the alternative minimum tax does not provide an intermediate, relatively less preferential rate for collectibles. Gains on collectibles are taxed at the normal alternative minimum tax rates.

The 2003 Act also added § 1(h)(11), under which dividends received by taxpayers other than corporations generally will be taxed at the same rate as long-term capital gains—15 percent for taxpayers otherwise taxable at a marginal rate greater than 15 percent (the 25 percent, 28 percent, 31 percent, and 35 percent brackets) and five percent for taxpayers otherwise taxed at a 10 or 15 percent marginal rate (with a special 0 percent rate for 10 and 15 percent bracket taxpayers in 2008). This result was achieved by treating dividends as "adjusted net capital gain" under § 1(h)(3), even though the dividend itself (in contrast to the stock) is not a capital asset as defined in § 1221, and dividends are not taken into account in the calculation of "net capital gain" under § 1222. Nevertheless, the statutory structure of § 55(b)(3)(B) and (C) results in extending the alternative minimum tax preferential rate for capital gains to dividends.

Page 1274:

After the first full paragraph, insert:

The individual alternative minimum tax originally was intended to apply primarily to taxpayers with significant economic income who because of tax preferences were paying little or no income taxes. Because of numerous amendments over the years to the alternative minimum tax, eliminating preferences, and to the regular income tax provisions, mostly the enactment of regular tax provisions specifically limiting tax-shelter deductions and credits, the individual alternative minimum tax currently does not significantly affect investors or unincorporated businesses. For 1997, five items that are "personal" in nature and not the result of tax planning strategies—personal exemptions, standard deductions, state and local tax deductions, medical expense deductions, and miscellaneous itemized deductions—collectively comprised 73.4 percent of individual alternative minimum tax preferences and adjustments. Studies indicate that, by 2007, almost 95 percent of the revenue from alternative minimum tax preferences and adjustments will be derived from the personal exemption, the standard deduction, state and local taxes, and miscellaneous itemized deductions. See Harvey & Tempalski, The Individual AMT: Why It Matters, 50 Nat. Tax J. 468 (1997); Tax Simplification Recommendations From ABA, AICPA, and TEI, LEXIS, TAXANA, 2000 TNT 39–82 (Feb. 28, 2000). As a result, the alternative minimum tax increasingly affects middle-income wage earners—taxpayers not engaged in tax-shelter or deferral strategies. In 2000 the percentage of taxpayers, grouped by adjusted gross income who were liable for the alternative minimum tax peaked in the range from $100,000 to $200,000 and thereafter steadily dropped. By 2010, the percentage of taxpayers liable for alternative minimum tax is projected to become significant in the $50,000 to $75,000 range, to peak in the $200,000 to $500,000 range, and thereafter to decline steeply. See Daniel Shaviro, Tax Simplification and the Alternative Minimum Tax, 91 Tax Notes 1455 (2001). A recent study by Treasury department economists suggests that, by 2010, 17 million individual taxpayers, nearly 16 percent of all taxpayers, will be subject to the alternative minimum tax. Robert Rebelein and Jerry Tempalski, Who Pays the Individual AMT?, U.S. Treasury Department, Office of Tax Analysis, OTA Paper 87 (June 2000), LEXIS, TAXANA, 2000 TNT 135–33. The Staff of the Joint Committee on Taxation estimates that, by 2010, 16.4 million taxpayers, many of whom Congress never intended to be subject to the alternative minimum tax, nevertheless will be liable for the alternative minimum tax. 2 Staff of the Joint Committee on Taxation, Study of the Overall State of the Federal Tax System and Recommendations for Simplification, Pursuant to Section 8022(3)(B) of the Internal Revenue Code of 1986, 13–14 (2001). Because the individual alternative minimum tax so widely misses its original mark, while adding inordinate complexity to the tax system for middle-income wage earners due to its interaction with limitations on the various personal credits, there is growing sentiment for its repeal, even among those who originally supported the enactment of the individual alternative minimum tax. The Staff of the Joint Committee on Taxation has recommended its repeal. Id. at 15–16.

APPENDIX

TIME VALUE OF MONEY: FUTURE AND PRESENT VALUES

Page 1278:

In the first full paragraph of text, lines seven and nine, replace "$100" **with** "$1,000".

†